Digital Photography
Top 100
2nd Edition

Simplified®

TIPS & TRICKS

by Gregory Georges

Visual

WILEY

Digital Photography: Top 100 Simplified® Tips & Tricks, Second Edition

Published by
Wiley Publishing, Inc.
111 River Street
Hoboken, NJ 07030-5774

Published simultaneously in Canada

Copyright © 2005 by Wiley Publishing, Inc., Indianapolis, Indiana

Library of Congress Control Number: 2005923205

ISBN-13: 978-0-7645-9616-2

ISBN-10: 0-7645-9616-0

Manufactured in the United States of America

10 9 8 7 6 5 4 3 2

2K/SV/QX/QV/IN

Trademark Acknowledgments

Contact Us

For general information on our other products and services, contact our Customer Care Department within the U.S. at 800-762-2974, outside the U.S. at 317-572-3993 or fax 317-572-4002.

For technical support, please visit www.wiley.com/techsupport.

WILEY
Wiley Publishing, Inc.

Sales

Contact Wiley at (800) 762-2974 or fax (317) 572-4002.

PRAISE FOR VISUAL BOOKS

"I have to praise you and your company on the fine products you turn out. I have twelve Visual books in my house. They were instrumental in helping me pass a difficult computer course. Thank you for creating books that are easy to follow. Keep turning out those quality books."

Gordon Justin (Brielle, NJ)

"What fantastic teaching books you have produced! Congratulations to you and your staff. You deserve the Nobel prize in Education. Thanks for helping me understand computers."

Bruno Tonon (Melbourne, Australia)

"A Picture Is Worth A Thousand Words! If your learning method is by observing or hands-on training, this is the book for you!"

Lorri Pegan-Durastante (Wickliffe, OH)

"Over time, I have bought a number of your 'Read Less - Learn More' books. For me, they are THE way to learn anything easily. I learn easiest using your method of teaching."

José A. Mazón (Cuba, NY)

"You've got a fan for life!! Thanks so much!!"

Kevin P. Quinn (Oakland, CA)

"I have several books from the Visual series and have always found them to be valuable resources."

Stephen P. Miller (Ballston Spa, NY)

"I have several of your Visual books and they are the best I have ever used."

Stanley Clark (Crawfordville, FL)

"Like a lot of other people, I understand things best when I see them visually. Your books really make learning easy and life more fun."

John T. Frey (Cadillac, MI)

"I have quite a few of your Visual books and have been very pleased with all of them. I love the way the lessons are presented!"

Mary Jane Newman (Yorba Linda, CA)

"Thank you, thank you, thank you...for making it so easy for me to break into this high-tech world."

Gay O'Donnell (Calgary, Alberta, Canada)

"I write to extend my thanks and appreciation for your books. They are clear, easy to follow, and straight to the point. Keep up the good work! I bought several of your books and they are just right! No regrets! I will always buy your books because they are the best."

Seward Kollie (Dakar, Senegal)

"I would like to take this time to thank you and your company for producing great and easy-to-learn products. I bought two of your books from a local bookstore, and it was the best investment I've ever made! Thank you for thinking of us ordinary people."

Jeff Eastman (West Des Moines, IA)

"Compliments to the chef!! Your books are extraordinary! Or, simply put, extra-ordinary, meaning way above the rest! THANKYOU THANKYOU THANKYOU! I buy them for friends, family, and colleagues."

Christine J. Manfrin (Castle Rock, CO)

CREDITS

Project Editor
Dana Rhodes Lesh

Acquisitions Editor
Jody Lefevere

Product Development Manager
Lindsay Sandman

Copy Editor
Dana Rhodes Lesh

Technical Editor
Lee Musick

Editorial Manager
Robyn Siesky

Editorial Assistant
Adrienne D. Porter

Manufacturing
Allan Conley
Linda Cook
Paul Gilchrist
Jennifer Guynn

Screen Artist
Jill A. Proll

Illustrator
Ronda David-Burroughs

Book Design
Kathie Rickard

Production Coordinator
Maridee V. Ennis

Layout
Joyce Haughey
Jennifer Heleine
Amanda Spagnuolo

Cover Design
Anthony Bunyan

Proofreader
Tammy Todd

Quality Control
Brian H. Walls

Indexer
Ty Koontz

**Vice President and Executive
Group Publisher**
Richard Swadley

Vice President and Publisher
Barry Pruett

Composition Director
Debbie Stailey

ABOUT THE AUTHOR

Gregory Georges is the author of the best-selling first edition of *Digital Photography: Top 100 Simplified Tips & Tricks,* as well as *50 Fast Digital Photo Techniques, 50 Fast Photoshop 7 Techniques,* and *50 Fast Digital Camera Techniques.* He has been an active photographer for over 25 years and a Photoshop expert since the early releases of the product. Over his career, he has taken pictures with medium format, 35mm, and digital cameras — resulting in a collection of over 15,000 images. Georges is also a contributing writer for *eDigitalPhoto* magazine, which is a new sister publication to *Shutterbug* magazine. Additionally, he has written articles for other magazines and content for a variety of vendors and Web sites to be used to promote his books.

HOW TO USE THIS BOOK

Digital Photography: Top 100 Simplified® Tips & Tricks, Second Edition, includes 100 tasks that reveal cool secrets, teach time-saving tricks, and explain great tips guaranteed to make you more productive with digital photography. The easy-to-use layout lets you work through all the tasks from beginning to end or jump in at random.

Who Is This Book For?

You already know the basics of digital photography. Now you would like to go beyond the basics, with shortcuts, tricks, and tips that enable you to work smarter and faster. And because you learn more easily when someone *shows* you how, this is the book for you.

Conventions Used in This Book

❶ Steps

This book uses step-by-step instructions to guide you easily through each task. Numbered callouts on every screen shot show you exactly how to perform each task, step by step.

❷ Tips

Practical tips provide insights to save you time and trouble, caution you about hazards to avoid, and reveal how to do things in digital photography that you never thought possible!

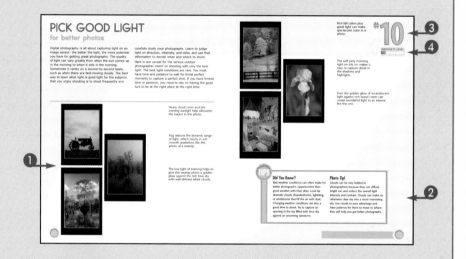

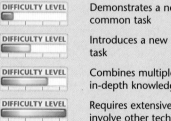

❸ Task Numbers

Task numbers from 1 to 100 indicate which lesson you are working on.

❹ Difficulty Levels

For quick reference, the symbols below mark the difficulty level of each task.

DIFFICULTY LEVEL	
	Demonstrates a new spin on a common task
	Introduces a new skill or a new task
	Combines multiple skills requiring in-depth knowledge
	Requires extensive skill and may involve other technologies

Table of Contents

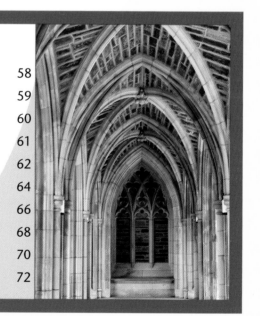

Table of Contents

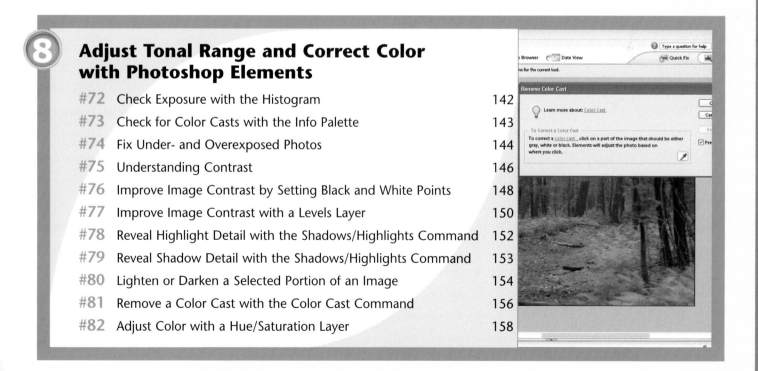

Table of Contents

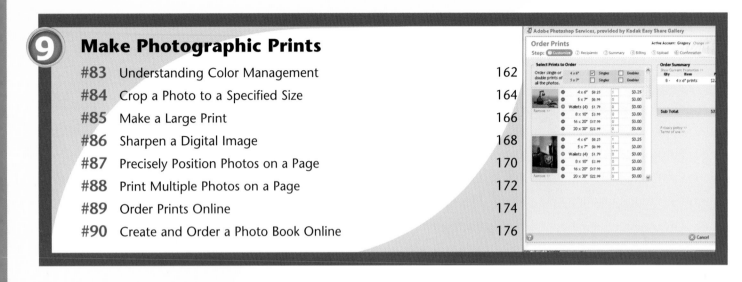
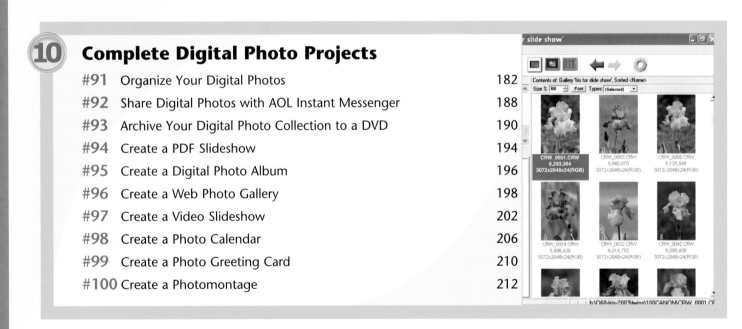

Chapter 1

Get Ready to Take Photos

Whether you are a snapshot photographer who takes several photos to record people, places, and events that are meaningful to you, or you are a passionate photographer who gets immense joy from making fine art photographs, you can always improve your photography if you do the right things before shooting.

Choosing what and where to shoot is the first step that you must take before shooting. Learn to find good events, places, and subjects to shoot by reading newspapers, books, or online resources. Look for good photo opportunities at local fairs, botanical gardens, nature preserves, national parks, or even zoos. Consider shooting still life or setting up a studio inside where you can control lighting.

When you know what you will be shooting, make sure that you know all that you can know about your digital camera. The more you know about your equipment, the more you can concentrate on getting the photographs that you want and not on learning how to use your camera. It can be very disappointing spending valuable time and money to take a trip only to find that you did not take good photos due to improper camera settings or usage.

When you go to shoot, be realistic; a day of shooting will not always result in one or more good photos. All photographers have bad days that end up with only mediocre photos — especially when the shooting conditions work against you!

Top 100

Select good
PHOTO OPPORTUNITIES

Unless you have specific reasons to shoot particular scenes or subjects, the best photo opportunities for you are those things that you enjoy. If you enjoy gardening and appreciate the thousands of different variations of iris, shoot irises. Or if you are a birdwatcher and find pleasure in watching wildlife, choose places where you can find birds and other wildlife in settings that make great photographs.

When planning a trip, give yourself plenty of time to stay and take photographs. Allow yourself some time for bad weather or other shooting conditions that prevent you from photographing. You can spend an entire day or more at a site and not have good enough light to shoot. Do not fall into the trap of trying to see too much too quickly. You may miss the kinds of shots that you had hoped to capture because you saw everything and shot little. Photography takes time, and time is often the most important factor in getting truly great photographs.

When shooting well-known places such as the Grand Canal in Venice or Canyon de Chelly in Arizona, take classic photos and then shoot creatively, too.

It took several hours of waiting to get a shadow on this otherwise overly bright photograph of the White House ruins in Canyon de Chelly in Arizona.

If you are willing to hike, you may be rewarded with photos that are well worth the effort that it took to get there.

This small backyard pond offers many subjects to photograph. Being close to home, it is easy to pick the best light to shoot in.

DIFFICULTY LEVEL

This frog was sunning on a rock on the edge of the pond shown in the preceding photo.

TIPS

Photo Tip!

When you find a good place to take photographs, visit it again and again. Your photographs will improve each time that you return to the location because you will learn when to visit and what to shoot.

Did You Know?

Some of the best photo opportunities may be in your own backyard. Learn to see differently and look for details, shapes, or colors that make good photographs — and then capture them.

Photo Tip!

Use the Internet to learn where and when to shoot. There are many online guides and forums that provide all the information you need to find wonderful places and subjects to shoot that will suit your interests.

KNOW WHY
you are taking photos

Should you shoot horizontally or vertically? If you have a choice of digital cameras, which one should you use? What camera settings will you use? Will your photographs be framed or displayed on a Web page? Are you going to display your photographs in a series, or should they be shot in a particular style? Are you shooting to get backgrounds or objects to include in another photograph? Do you plan to digitally edit your photographs with an image editor such as Adobe Photoshop after you take them?

Your answers to these questions and others like them will have a substantial impact on how you should shoot. Knowing why you are taking photos before you take them can help you get the photos that you want. For example, suppose you make a once-in-a-lifetime trip and get excellent pictures. You then decide to make a calendar but cannot find enough photos to fit the horizontal format that you have chosen. Thinking about why you are taking the photographs and how they are likely to be viewed can help you to better plan your photographs.

This photo of a green anole was taken so that it could be used in a variety of media.

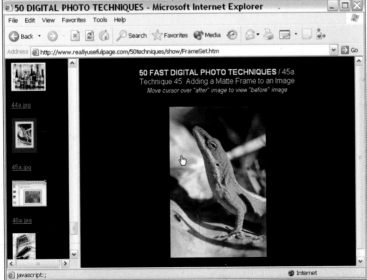

Minor cropping enables the photo to be displayed in a Web browser-based photo gallery.

Vertical orientation and composition makes it possible to frame this photo in standard-sized photo frames and mat boards.

Good cover design allowed the leaf on the left side of the photo to be used for the magazine's cover text.

TIPS

Photo Tip!

When you know that you will share a photo online, you can take advantage of the "multiplication factor" that you get when you crop an image from a large image. A small bird in a mostly blue sky print can become a large bird that fills the frame when it is cropped for the Web.

Did You Know?

Custom-sized frames and mat boards can be considerably more expensive than those of standard sizes. When possible, you should consider shooting so that you can use standard 4" x 6", 5" x 7", 8" x 10", and 11" x 14" frames and mat boards.

Did You Know?

A good photograph for the cover of a magazine usually needs to be shot vertically with some space on the photo where text and graphics may be placed without interfering with the composition of the subject.

MASTER YOUR CAMERA
to get great photos

Today's sophisticated digital cameras enable anyone to take good, and sometimes great, photographs by simply using one of the automatic shooting modes and pressing the shutter release. However, most digital cameras offer many additional features that give serious photographers considerable creative control over how photos are taken and ensure that a higher percentage of photos are taken as you want them.

One major advantage of most digital cameras is that you can review the image and camera settings on an LCD screen immediately after taking the photo. This enables you to check that you have composed the photo as you like and that the camera settings were set as you expected. Some digital cameras even provide a *histogram* to give you a graphical view of the exposure. These review features are well worth using.

To get the best photos, learn all that you can about your digital camera. You must master your camera, or it will limit your success.

This dial on a Canon PowerShot G2 controls the shooting modes.

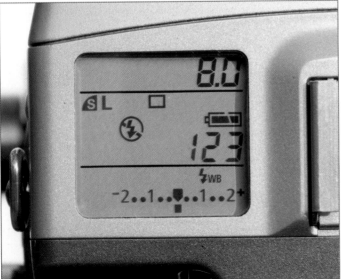

The Canon PowerShot G2 LCD screen shows important camera settings at a glance.

8

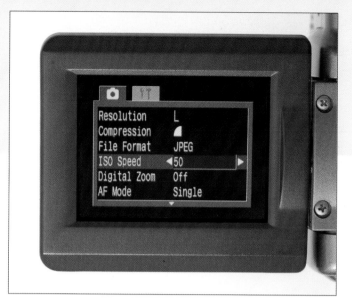

Important camera settings are controlled on the Canon PowerShot G2 via multiple menus.

The LCD screen on the Canon PowerShot G2 shows a screen with camera settings, a histogram, and a thumbnail image.

Did You Know?

The more you learn about and use different features on your camera, the more likely it will be that you will forget which settings you have changed and will shoot using the wrong settings. Learn how to quickly check your settings or to set them to the default settings in order to avoid shooting with the wrong settings. Many photos are ruined because of improper camera settings. The most common settings that cause problems are exposure compensation, white balance, auto-ISO change, and image size.

Caution!

Many digital cameras have shooting modes that automatically choose a faster ISO setting (see Task #6) if there is not sufficient light. Make sure that you know which shooting modes allow this to avoid taking photos that have too much digital noise.

CHOOSE THE IMAGE FILE FORMAT
to suit your needs

Each time that you press the shutter release, you capture an image on the image sensor. The image is then written to a file in a user-selected format with or without your chosen camera settings being applied. Most digital cameras offer three formats: JPEG (.jpg), TIFF (.tif), and RAW format.

The most commonly used format is the JPEG format. It offers a nice balance between image file size and image quality. The JPEG format is a *lossy* format; it uses a mathematical algorithm to reduce the file size while losing minimal image quality. The TIFF format is a *nonlossy* format, which means that no image quality is lost, but files are also considerably larger.

Unlike JPEG and TIFF files, RAW image files are proprietary files that do not have most of the camera settings applied to them. For greater creative flexibility, the photographer can use a RAW image converter, such as Adobe Camera RAW (see Task #61), and apply camera settings to the files *after* the photos have been taken.

RAW format images are digital "negatives" that need to be converted to be viewed and edited.

These file sizes are from a Nikon CoolPix 5700. File sizes from other digital cameras will vary.

Approximate Image File Sizes			
Image Size	*TIFF*	*JPEG*	*RAW*
5-Megapixel Image	14.5MB	1.5MB	7.8MB
Compression Ratio	1:1	10:1	2:1

JPEG versus RAW File Format	
JPEG	**RAW**
- All camera settings are applied to the file	+ Image stored as captured by sensor, allowing post-shoot changes
+ Smaller file size	- Larger file size
+ Easily viewable images	- Requires RAW conversion software
+ Quick to view	- Slower to view
- 8-bit image (less picture information)	+ Wider bit range (12 or 14 bits yield more picture information)

TIPS

Did You Know?

The RAW format is the best image format to use if you want to get the best possible pictures from your digital camera. Camera settings such as white balance, contrast, saturation levels, sharpening, and other settings are not applied to a RAW image file. After you shoot, you have control over these settings when processing them with a RAW image converter such as Adobe Camera RAW (see Task #61) or one provided by your camera manufacturer. Many serious photographers shoot in RAW format most of the time.

Did You Know?

RAW image file converters enable you to change exposure compensation to your photos after you have taken them by up to plus or minus two f-stops! That alone makes it worthwhile to shoot in RAW format.

Set the
IMAGE RESOLUTION AND COMPRESSION LEVEL

In addition to letting you choose a file format for your photos, most digital cameras enable you to choose the image resolution. If you have chosen the JPEG file format, many cameras also enable you to specify the compression level. Image resolution is expressed in terms of pixels, such as 2,560 x 1,920 pixels. If you multiply these two numbers together, you get the total pixel count — for example, 2,560 x 1,920 = 4,915,200, or just about 5 megapixels. More pixels in a picture enable you to print a larger print, which is the primary reason to buy a more expensive digital camera with a higher megapixel rating.

There is a tradeoff, however, between the number of pixels and the image file size — the more pixels, the larger the file. To fit more digital photos on digital photo storage media, the JPEG file format enables you to select the level of compression, which reduces file size. Unfortunately, the more an image is compressed, the lower the image quality. To choose the optimal settings for your photography, you need to balance the tradeoffs between image size (resolution), compression level, image quality, and possible print size.

This photo was taken with a 3.1-megapixel camera with an image size of 2,160 x 1,440 pixels.

This 800 x 600 pixel image was taken from the center of the preceding image. It makes an excellent "full-size" Web page photo.

Print Size		
Megapixels	**Image Resolution**	**Print Size***
2	1,200 x 1,600	5" x 6.7"
3	1,512 x 2,016	6.3" x 8.4"
4	1,704 x 2,272	7.1" x 9.5"
5	1,944 x 2,592	8.1" x 10.8"
6	2,048 x 3,072	8.5" x 12.8"

* This assumes that the optimal printing is 240PPI. Good images and proper image editing techniques may allow considerably larger prints to be made.

DIFFICULTY LEVEL

TIPS

Did You Know?

By reducing the image resolution to store more photos, you lose the benefits of image cropping and the ability to get a larger print later. As digital photo storage media prices continue to drop, you can buy one or more extra cards so that you can store your images at the maximum image resolution and with the least image compression. This decision enables you to avoid getting a prized shot that is too small or has too much compression to make a good print.

Did You Know?

Each time you save a JPEG file after editing it, your image degrades. Therefore, if you need to open, edit, and save a JPEG image more than once, you should save all but the final images in an uncompressed image format such as TIFF, bitmap (.bmp), or Photoshop (.psd).

CONTROL YOUR CAMERA'S LIGHT SENSITIVITY
with the ISO setting

In traditional film photography, you choose film based upon an *ISO rating* (the new term for the *ASA setting*), such as ISO 100 or ISO 400, depending on how much light you expect to have when you shoot. Photographers consider film with a low ISO rating such as ISO 100 to be a slower film than ISO 400 because it takes a longer shutter speed to properly expose the film than film with a higher ISO rating, which enables an image to be recorded more quickly.

Digital cameras also enable you to change the ISO setting between each shot. Choosing an ISO setting is one of the most important settings that you can make. Although a faster ISO setting, such as ISO 400 or 800, enables you to shoot in lower-light settings without image blur due to long exposure times, you will end up with considerably more digital noise in your digital photos. Digital noise is similar to grain in traditional photography and is generally an undesirable tradeoff that you get when using higher ISO settings.

This photo was shot at ISO 800 to enable a faster shutter speed, avoiding image blur in the low light.

Digital noise is easily visible in most of this photo.

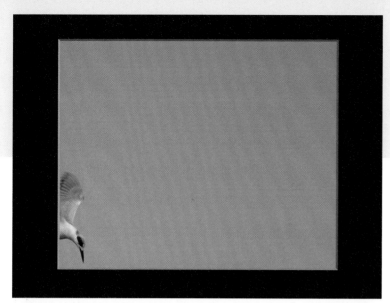

No digital noise appears in this photo, which was shot at ISO 100.

ISO 800 was used to achieve a traditional film grain effect in this black-and-white photo.

TIPS

Did You Know?

You generally get the best picture quality by using the lowest ISO setting your camera offers, such as ISO 50 or 100. A higher setting such as ISO 400 or 800 will have considerably more digital noise.

Photo Tip!

Although digital noise is generally an unwanted characteristic of a digital photo, you can use it as a creative design element. Digital noise gives a photo a grainy effect similar to the grain found in traditional photographic prints.

Did You Know?

When you edit a digital photo with an image editor, such as Adobe Photoshop Elements, you are likely to get more pronounced digital noise when you perform steps such as increasing contrast, increasing image size, and sharpening an image.

Improve color with the
WHITE BALANCE SETTING

One of the more significant challenges facing digital photographers is to take photographs with accurate color. A common problem is getting a photo that has an undesirable *color cast,* which means that the photo has too much of a certain color, such as red, blue, or green. An improper white balance setting often causes this problem. An in-camera white balance setting enables you to record correct colors when shooting under a variety of different lighting conditions such as incandescent light, tungsten light, sunshine, or clouds.

Besides letting you choose an appropriate white balance setting, many digital cameras have a custom white balance setting that can record very accurate colors after you first take a photo of a white card. If your camera offers such a feature, it is worth learning about and using. One of the more consistent ways to get accurate color is to shoot in RAW mode, which enables you to change the white balance setting using a RAW converter long after you take the photo. Most RAW converters, such as Adobe Camera RAW, have controls that can be used to fine-tune the white balance (see Task #61).

This photo was taken outdoors on a cloudy day with the white balance set incorrectly to tungsten.

This photo was taken outdoors on a cloudy day with the white balance set correctly to cloudy.

This photo was taken outdoors on a cloudy day with the camera's white balance set to auto white balance.

This photo was taken outdoors on a cloudy day using the RAW format, which enabled the photographer to select accurate color after the shot was taken.

Although accurate color means that white is pure white, sometimes you want a color cast such as the golden glow of sunset found in this cat photo.

TIPS

Photo Tip!

Sometimes you can add a preset white balance setting to add a favorable color tone to a photo. For example, using a cloudy white balance setting can add warmth to an otherwise cold or blue-toned scene.

Did You Know?

Most digital image editors offer several color-correction tools. However, many of them work best if you have a pure white or neutral gray tone in your image. When you are concerned about getting accurate color and you do not have a pure white or neutral gray tone in the composition, consider placing a white card in the photo. After you use the white area for color correction purposes, you can remove it with your digital image editor.

Shoot for
DIGITAL EDITING

Taking a photograph with a digital camera is one small part — albeit a significant part — of the entire digital photography process. If you shoot digitally without considering the possibilities of what you can do later in an image editor, you will dramatically limit your creativity and your picture-making ability.

To take advantage of the new world of digital photography, you should become as familiar with an image editor such as Adobe Photoshop Elements as you are with your camera. Learn how your image editor enables you to combine, fix, distort, correct, tint, or otherwise change your photos to become

more than they were. Digitally stitching multiple images together into a single panoramic photograph, increasing tonal range and image contrast, and creating photographs with a full dynamic range are just a few of the wonders you can achieve when you become proficient with an image editor.

Although a digital image editor provides you with tremendous image-manipulation power, do not forget that you can always do more with well-taken photos than you can with marginally acceptable ones. Great image editing always begins with an excellent photograph.

This photo of tree bark was taken to use as a background for another photo.

This simple photo of a tree was taken to combine with a background photo.

This image was made by combining the two preceding photos.

Adobe Photoshop Elements filters and plug-ins were used to create this painting-like image of the tree.

A row of old trucks was transformed into this image with Adobe Photoshop.

#8

Five separate photos were combined to create this image of kids and seagulls flying over the coast.

TIPS

Photo Tip!

After you have purchased a digital camera and some digital photo storage media, taking photos does not cost anything, so shoot often — and then shoot again. Learn to try different exposure settings and compositions, and shoot plenty of shots so that you have a choice between several good ones.

Did You Know?

You can use an image editor like Adobe Photoshop Elements to remove or add photographic elements such as telephone lines, sky, clouds, people, and so on. If you have composed a photo that has a distracting element, shoot anyway and fix it later in your image editor (see Task #63). Just remember that it is usually easier to shoot a photo that does not need correction in an image editor than it is to have to edit it later.

PACK
for a successful and enjoyable shoot

Patiently waiting is often a key part of photography. Depending on your shooting conditions, you may have to wait for better light, less or more rain, a subject to appear, a cloud to move, or even the sun to rise or set. In any event, patience can be the most important personality trait a photographer can have to get good photographs. The best way to strengthen that trait is to bring along items that will make your outing more enjoyable, productive, and safe.

If you are too hot or too cold, hungry, or tired, or you are being bitten by bugs, you are likely to take fewer good photos than if you are happy and comfortable. Before you head off for a shoot, carefully consider what you should take with you in addition to your photography equipment. A few nutrition bars, water, a lightweight folding chair, sunscreen, and a hat can unquestionably contribute to your taking better photographs.

A lightweight folding tripod chair makes it easy for this photographer to quietly wait for a bullfrog to pop his head above water.

Water, sunscreen, insect repellent and bite medication, and snacks are just a few things that will make your picture-taking time more enjoyable.

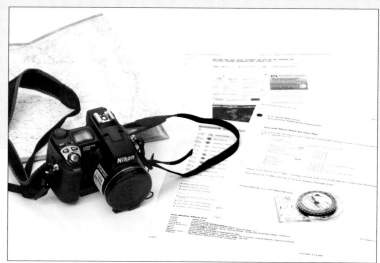

A compass and a schedule of sunrise and sunset and the moon's path will make it easier for you to be in the right place at the right time to get great photographs.

Take a hat to protect yourself from the sun and use a headlamp, such as the Princeton-Tec headlamp, to make your walks safe when walking in the dark.

TIP

Did You Know?

Some of the most useful information for photographers is found on the Internet.

Sunrise/Sunset/Twilight/Moonrise/Moonset/Phase information: http://aa.usno.navy.mil/data/docs/RS_OneDay.html

Weather: www.weather.com or www.weatherbug.com

Hiking equipment: www.rei.com

Online mapping service: www.mapquest.com

Best state parks: http://usparks.about.com/cs/stateparks/a/bestparks.htm

All-encompassing outdoor page: http://gorp.com

Chapter 2

Choose Good Light

Although your natural inclination may be to focus your attention on your subject and compose carefully to get the shots you want, you can greatly improve your photography if you put an equal amount of time into evaluating and controlling light. What often distinguishes really good photographs from all the rest is how light is used to capture the photograph. Depending on the kinds of subjects you shoot, you may need to work exclusively with natural light, or you may be able to use a combination of natural and artificial light.

After you have decided what you want to shoot and you have a vision for the kind of shots you want, carefully consider the characteristics of the available light if you are shooting with natural light. Do you have backlighting or front lighting, or does the light come in from the side? Does the light come in from a low angle, or is the sun high in the sky? Is the light soft and diffused, or is it bright and intense? Does the light have a nice, warm golden glow or maybe an unwanted color cast?

When you do not have good light, consider ways in which you may improve it, or find another time to try again. Can you use one or more flashes? Are you shooting close-ups when a macro ring light may be the most effective kind of supplemental light? Would one or more handheld light reflectors be useful? The more you take advantage of quality light, the better your photos will be.

Top 100

PICK GOOD LIGHT
for better photos

Digital photography is all about capturing light on an image sensor; the better the light, the more potential you have for getting great photographs. The quality of light can vary greatly from when the sun comes up in the morning to when it sets in the evening. Sometimes it varies on a second-by-second basis, such as when there are fast-moving clouds. A good way to learn what light is best for the subjects that you enjoy shooting is to shoot frequently and carefully study your photographs. Learn to judge light on direction, intensity, and color, and use that information to decide when and where to shoot.

Here is one caveat for the serious outdoor photographer intent on shooting with only the best light: The best light conditions are rare. You must have time and patience to wait for those perfect moments to capture a perfect shot. If you have limited time or patience, you need to rely on having enough luck to be at the right place at the right time.

Heavy cloud cover and late evening sunlight help silhouette the tractor in this photo.

Fog reduces the dynamic range of light, which results in soft smooth gradations like this photo of a swamp.

The low light of evening helps to give this swamp photo a golden glow against the rich blue sky with well-defined white clouds.

Rich fall colors plus the right light can make spectacular color in a photo.

The soft, early morning light on this iris makes it easy to capture detail in the shadows and highlights.

Even the golden glow of incandescent light against rich wood colors can create wonderful light in an interior like this one.

Did You Know?

Bad weather conditions can often make for better photographic opportunities than good weather with blue skies. Look for dramatic clouds, thunderstorms, lightning, or windstorms that fill the air with dust. Changing weather conditions are also a good time to shoot. Try to capture an opening in the sky filled with blue sky against an oncoming rainstorm.

Photo Tip!

Clouds can be very helpful to photographers because they can diffuse bright sun and reduce the overall light intensity and contrast. Clouds can make an otherwise clear sky a little more interesting. Use clouds to your advantage and have patience for them to move to where they will help you get better photographs.

Shoot in
HAZE OR FOG

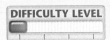

DIFFICULTY LEVEL

Do not avoid taking photos just because there is haze or fog. Haze or fog can act as an excellent light diffuser that can help you to get some wonderful photos. Besides helping to reduce the overall contrast of an image, haze or fog can create an atmosphere that may transform what would otherwise be an uninteresting scene into a beautiful photograph.

When properly exposing haze or fog, you can get stunning silhouettes and smooth monotone gradations that can make a photograph both simple and powerful. Haze or fog can also add some mystery to a photo, as a viewer may not be able to see much detail in the photograph. Whenever you have a chance to shoot in haze or fog, take it. Make sure, however, that you understand how to use exposure compensation because your camera's built-in light meter will likely give you an exposure that is not what you want. For a detailed explanation of exposure compensation, see Task #25.

You can use a digital image editor such as Adobe Photoshop Elements to further refine your haze or fog photos into spectacular images.

The haze seen from the Smoky Mountains makes photographs like this one rich in soft subtle gradations that diminish with distance.

The fog in this swamp combines with the late evening sun to help create wonderful, monotone silhouettes of trees in the water.

SILHOUETTE
your subject

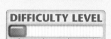
DIFFICULTY LEVEL

Backlighting occurs when your subject has a bright light in back of it, often resulting in dark shadows on the subject. Shooting in this kind of lighting can be both challenging and rewarding. The often extreme contrast between the bright background and an unlit subject makes it possible to get a silhouette.

Getting a good exposure in a backlit situation can be difficult. Shoot a couple of photos with different settings and compare the results on your camera's LCD screen. If your camera offers a histogram (see Task #24), you can use it to see if you have a dark

or nearly black silhouetted subject or if you have blown-out highlights (see Task #26) in the bright areas of the composition.

After you have taken a silhouette, you can use an image editor such as Adobe Photoshop Elements to further refine the image and turn it into an excellent print. You can use the Set Black Point eyedropper tool found in the Levels dialog box to make the silhouetted subject pure black by selecting the eyedropper and clicking the area that is silhouetted.

The fading sunlight behind the trees produced this silhouette.

Underexposure caused this silhouette of a flying pelican, but it makes a nice photo anyway.

Learn when to shoot with a
BUILT-IN FLASH

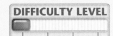

DIFFICULTY LEVEL

A camera with a built-in flash is very useful when you take snapshots or when there is not enough light and you cannot add light in any other way. Otherwise, you should carefully consider ways to avoid using a built-in flash most of the time. A built-in flash lights your subject with unnatural light that comes straight from the camera. The resulting effect is that important shadows, which add dimension to your subject, are removed by the flash. The use of an external flash has the benefit of projecting light on a subject from an angle that helps maintain important subtle shadows.

If your camera has *flash exposure compensation,* which enables you to reduce the balance of flash relative to natural light, you can use a *fill flash* (see Task #14) to lighten some of the darker shadows to reveal details while keeping some shadow to add dimension to the subject. You can also use a built-in flash to provide a *catch light* (see Task #15) to any subject with eyes and to stop motion.

This photo taken without a flash shows good dimension and natural colors.

The use of a built-in flash for this photo has diminished the shadows, resulting in a flat-looking image with less natural colors.

Reveal detail with a
FILL FLASH

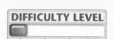

DIFFICULTY LEVEL

A *fill flash* is light from a built-in or external flash that is used to illuminate dark shadows to reveal detail and to reduce overall image contrast in bright sun. When you are shooting compositions with strong shadows or backlighting, consider using a fill flash.

When you shoot a backlit subject and the primary light source is behind your subject and in front of you, the result can be an extremely high contrast. A fill flash can reduce the image contrast while lighting your subject to reveal important details. Most backlit subjects are challenging to meter, so try a few different flash and exposure settings to get the photo that you want.

If your camera has exposure compensation, you can use that feature to get the best balance between existing light and light from the flash. The closer you are to the subject, the more important it is to use exposure compensation to reduce the overall power of your flash so that you do not overwhelm your subject with bright artificial light.

This is a Canon 550EX Speedlite mounted on a Canon PowerShot G2.

Bright sun creates extreme contrast on this iris with well-lit areas and dark flat shadow areas.

A fill flash reduces the overall contrast and lights the shadowy areas to reveal detail in the iris.

Add a catch light to your
SUBJECTS' EYES

Generally, whenever you are shooting a subject with eyes, you should try to keep the eyes in focus and capture a sparkle or *catch light* in them. Without a catch light, your subjects will look lifeless and considerably less attractive than if they had this tiny, but very important, feature.

Often lighting conditions enable you to shoot with existing light and get a catch light. If you are shooting without the benefit of light that enables you to get a catch light, use a flash or other light source.

To avoid adding too much artificial light from a flash, use flash compensation if it is available on your camera or an external flash to reduce the balance of light from the flash relative to ambient light. The distance to the subject and the power of the flash are important variables to consider when setting the flash exposure compensation. What you do not want to do is ruin your intended natural lighting just to add a catch light to the eyes.

This child's portrait was greatly enhanced with a flash to add a catch light to the eyes.

This close-up photo shows the important catch light, or sparkle light, in the child's eyes.

Prevent
RED EYE

The dreaded *red eye* is caused by light from a flash reflected back from a subject's retina to the camera. Sadly, unnatural red eyes almost always ruin the resulting photograph. To avoid getting photographs whose subjects have red eyes, many camera vendors have added features that are known as *red-eye reduction features.* Although these features can reduce or eliminate red eye, they often create other problems. The best strategy is to learn how to shoot without using a red-eye reduction feature.

To avoid getting red eye, you simply need to shoot so that the angle between the flash and lens to the subject's eyes is more than five degrees. Using an off-camera flash is one way to avoid getting red eye. You can also have your subjects look away from the camera slightly, or you can find a shooting environment or use camera settings that do not require a flash. You are more likely to get red eye when shooting in a dark environment because the pupil will be wider and more prone to reflect red light.

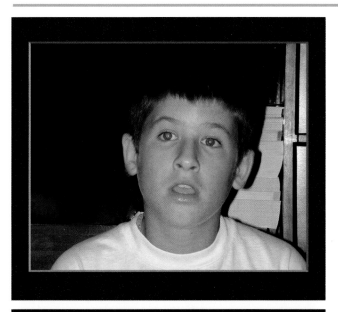

In this photograph, you can see the dreaded red eye caused by a flash.

Red eye can even occur in the eyes of pets and wildlife subjects, such as this great horned owl.

ADD NATURAL LIGHT
with a reflector

One useful and inexpensive photographic accessory is a light reflector, such as the 32" Stroboframe Pops portable light modifier, which costs under $35. You can use it to reflect soft natural light toward your subject and as a shade cover to reduce overly bright and high contrast direct sunlight. Most similar portable light reflectors fold up to one-third of their open size, and they usually offer a white side and a second colored side such as silver, gold, or bronze.

A handheld light reflector is especially useful for adding light to a subject's face for a portrait. Besides filling shadows with natural light, you can add a warm color tone by using a bronze- or gold-colored side of the reflector. When shooting a backlit subject, a reflective light modifier, such as the Stroboframe light modifier, is an excellent tool to use to add natural fill light to the subject to reveal greater detail.

Stroboframe light modifiers and similar products are available in multiple sizes and are easy to pack and carry in the field.

This portrait was taken in bright direct sun with a Stroboframe light modifier to reduce contrast and to evenly light the face. Notice the absence of harsh shadows.

Here, the Stroboframe light modifier is held to reflect light up toward the face of the model.

This wildflower photograph was taken on a bright sunny day under the shade created by a Stroboframe light modifier.

DIFFICULTY LEVEL

The photographer is using a self-timer and a Stroboframe light modifier to shade and photograph a wildflower.

TIPS

Did You Know?

Large white mat boards, which can be purchased at most art stores, make excellent inexpensive light reflectors. Although they are not as convenient to store and carry as collapsible light modifiers, such as the Stroboframe Pops light modifier, they can be used to reflect light where it is needed. One advantage to using a white reflector over an additional light source is that it will not alter the color temperature of the ambient lighting, which can occur when using an artificial light source.

Apply It!

If you have only a single strobe or hot light and you need to have light coming from a second direction, you can use a reflector to bounce light back from the flash to the subject. Just place the reflector opposite the light and reflect the light back to the subject to get an evenly lit subject.

SHOOT CLOSE-UPS
with a macro ring light

If you are serious about taking close-up, or macro, photographs, consider getting a macro ring light. A *macro ring light* is a flash that attaches to and wraps around the front of a macro lens. Although a macro ring light can light up shadows in such a way that the subject loses some definition, a skilled photographer can alter the ratio of the light coming from the two lights to maintain realistic shadows. Most macro ring lights also have a modeling light that is useful for both seeing your subject and providing enough light for your camera to auto-focus.

A macro ring light is also extremely valuable when you want to increase depth of field. Whenever you shoot close to a subject, you have a limited depth of field. To maximize depth of field, you need to choose a small aperture, which means that you will have a longer exposure. Long exposures allow small movements in the subject to record as a blurred subject. Using a flash, you can freeze the subject movement while benefiting from the increased depth of field, resulting in perfectly focused and exposed subjects.

A Canon MR-14EX TTL Macro Ring Lite flash is mounted on the front of a Canon PowerShot G2.

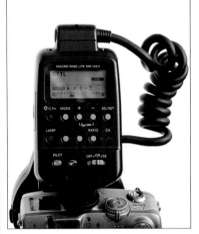

The Canon MR-14EX TTL Macro Ring Lite flash offers many features and controls for taking well-lit photos.

The interior details of this blue and yellow iris are well lit by a macro ring light.

A macro ring light provides excellent light for this spider with a catch light in the eyes.

18

DIFFICULTY LEVEL

This close-up shot even shows detail in the cornea of the turtle's eye. This shot would have been difficult to light without a macro ring light.

Did You Know?

When you shoot close-up or macro photographs, you should use a tripod. A tripod helps you accurately focus your photographs and more precisely control the depth of field and composition.

Caution!

Vendors other than the major camera vendors make several excellent macro ring lights. However, be careful if you decide to purchase a macro ring light manufactured by a vendor other than the one that made your camera. You may not be able to use all the features. A good but more expensive option is to buy a macro ring light from your camera manufacturer.

Illuminate portraits with
WINDOW LIGHT

Getting a good portrait is highly dependent on the quality and quantity of light that is available. That is one of the reasons why so many portrait photographers strongly prefer to shoot inside a photography studio where they have the most control over lighting. One of the most useful lighting accessories in a portrait studio is a *soft box,* which is a large light box that diffuses the light from a flash to make soft, even, natural-looking light for well-lit portraits.

You can get the same soft, evenly diffused light in your own home without the expense of having a studio with studio flash and soft boxes by shooting portraits with the subject standing in front of a window. Depending on the light, you can either shoot with the light coming in directly through the window, or you can use the diffused light that comes through a white sheer drape. If you want to control the background, you can have your subjects hold a mat board up behind them.

You can create an excellent portrait by positioning your subjects in front of a window while they hold a mat board behind them as a background.

This portrait was taken using natural light shining in through a window.

Take advantage of the
GOLDEN HOUR

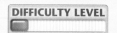
DIFFICULTY LEVEL

The best sunlight is often found an hour or less before sunset until 20 or so minutes past sunset. This time is often referred to as the *golden hour* for photographers. When light is low in the sky, it gives you a very directional light that adds wonderful depth to your photographs because of the shadows that it creates. The evening light is also usually warmer and richer in color than early morning light. If you shoot landscape photos, this is a time that you will rarely want to miss.

When you plan on taking advantage of the sun in the golden hour, be well prepared to shoot quickly because the best of that time may come and go in just a few minutes. Make sure that you have all your equipment out, set up, and ready to shoot, or you will have to wait for the next sunset. You should also wait 20 minutes past sunset for any possible afterglow, which occasionally makes for a spectacular landscape photograph, so do not pack up and leave too soon.

The golden hour of sunset casts a wonderful color on these reeds near the edge of the water.

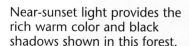

Near-sunset light provides the rich warm color and black shadows shown in this forest.

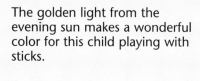

The golden light from the evening sun makes a wonderful color for this child playing with sticks.

Chapter 3

Control Exposure

Although many factors contribute to making a good photograph, one of the most important factors is exposure. Even though your camera's light meter can help you choose the right combination of shutter speed and aperture, and in some cases even the ISO speed, it can still misread the amount of light and give you a photo unlike what you have in mind. To improve your chances of getting the exposure you want, most digital cameras offer a wide range of features that can help considerably. Understanding features such as exposure metering modes, histograms, and exposure compensation and understanding how to use manual mode can help you get the exposure that you want.

Even the challenge of capturing the full range of brightness, from the darkest darks to the brightest highlights, is easier if you understand what you can do later with an image editor on your computer and you plan for combining two or more images. When it comes to getting the right exposure, the digital camera wins hands down over the film camera. Not only do you have all the incredibly useful features to help you get the right exposure, but you can instantly see the image on an LCD panel. If you are not happy with the picture that you took, you can shoot until you get what you want — and it does not cost a thing!

Top 100

UNDERSTANDING EXPOSURE
to get the photos that you want

Exposure is the correct combination of shutter speed, aperture, and ISO speed to get the photograph that you want. Exposure can be determined solely by the camera, by you (as the photographer) and the camera together, or solely by you. Whenever the camera helps you choose exposure settings, the camera's built-in light meter takes a reading of the reflected light in the scene and then selects the appropriate camera settings.

When taking photos, remember that there is no such thing as a *perfect* exposure — only one that is how you want it to be. Overexposed photographs are overly light, and detail is lost in the highlights. Underexposed photos are overly dark, and detail is lost in the shadows.

Because digital camera exposure metering systems measure light as if it were reflected from a neutral-gray surface, they may misread the light when a scene is very dark or very light. Classic examples include a black cat sitting in front of a large pile of black coal or a white cat sitting on snow.

UNDEREXPOSED
Underexposing this photograph led to a loss of detail in the shadow area.

PROPERLY EXPOSED
This well-exposed photograph reveals details in the highlight areas and in the shadow areas.

OVEREXPOSED
Overexposing, or "washing out," this photograph lost detail in the cloud area.

This photo was not metered correctly, and as a result, the dark black cat appears gray.

#21

DIFFICULTY LEVEL

This photo of two white cats shown against a black background was metered incorrectly, and the white cats appear gray.

Photographers often incorrectly meter scenes with a lot of white sand or snow, as is the case with this underexposed photo of a snow-covered dairy farm.

TIPS

Did You Know?

One of the significant advantages of using the RAW format (see Task #4), if it is available on your digital camera, is that RAW conversion tools enable you to vary the exposure by +/– two f-stops. If you plan on using this feature, make sure that you do not overexpose the image and "blow out" the highlights (see Task #26) because you will not be able to retrieve picture information in that area with a RAW conversion tool. See Task #61 for more information on the RAW format.

Photo Tip!

If you are shooting in a format other than RAW or you are shooting a scene that may not be metered correctly, consider using the *auto-bracketing* feature if it is available on your camera. Auto-bracketing enables you to shoot three sequential shots; the camera will automatically shoot at a user-selected + and – stop increment around the metered setting.

Discover different
EXPOSURE MODES

Most digital cameras offer a variety of exposure modes, including program or auto mode, shutter priority, aperture priority, manual, and bulb (time) modes. Choosing an exposure mode determines which exposure settings you can select and which, if any, exposure settings the camera will automatically select based on the settings that you have selected.

The camera automatically chooses both shutter speed and aperture settings when you select the program or automatic mode. When using these modes on some cameras, you can sometimes modify these initial "camera-chosen" settings.

When you select the shutter priority mode, the camera automatically chooses the aperture setting to get a good exposure. Likewise, when you choose the aperture priority mode, you choose the aperture setting that you want, and the camera will select the appropriate shutter speed. Remember to choose the shutter speed setting when using shutter priority mode and to choose the aperture setting when you use the aperture priority mode; otherwise, you will simply be using the last setting that was used. In situations in which you want complete control over both shutter speed and aperture, choose the manual mode.

GENERAL EXPOSURE MODES

You usually select an exposure mode by turning a dial like this one found on the Canon PowerShot G2.

For snapshot photos and general use, select program or automatic exposure mode.

DIFFICULTY LEVEL

PRIORITY MODES

Choose the aperture priority mode when you want to control depth of field; in this mode, the camera automatically sets its shutter speed.

Choose shutter priority mode when you want to control shutter speed; the camera then automatically sets the aperture.

MANUAL MODE

Use manual mode when you want complete control over both shutter speed and aperture.

TIPS

Did You Know?

Automatic shooting modes such as landscape, macro, and portrait modes often result in a good photograph. However, they are not likely to produce photos as good as you can get if you understand and correctly use the shutter priority or aperture priority mode settings.

Caution!

Some shooting modes such as program or automatic mode allow the camera to automatically change the ISO setting if a change is needed. When you use a faster ISO speed, there will be more digital noise in the image. If you do not want to have excess digital noise, make sure that you know when to avoid using a mode that causes automatic ISO speed changes.

Choose an appropriate
METERING MODE

Today's digital cameras have a built-in exposure meter that measures the amount of reflected light from a scene to determine the appropriate settings to get a medium-toned exposure. Although built-in exposure meters are getting increasingly sophisticated, they can take readings that do not provide the exposures that you want. In many cases, these "bad" readings are caused by reading either too much or too little light from the scene. To give you more control over what light is metered, most digital cameras offer more than one exposure meter mode.

Some of the more common exposure meter modes are *averaging* or *multisegment, center-weighted,* and *spot.* The most useful is the averaging or multisegment mode, which takes a reading from the entire area shown in your composition. The center-weighted mode places more emphasis on the center of the image, and spot metering reads only a tiny part of the image. Picking the most appropriate exposure metering mode increases the chance that you will get the exposure you want.

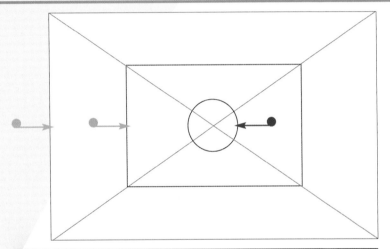

- This area is read by the averaging, or multisegment, metering mode.

- This area is read by the centered-weighted metering mode.

- This area is read by the spot metering mode.

The averaging, or multisegment, metering mode is well suited for most images like this scene showing farm trucks.

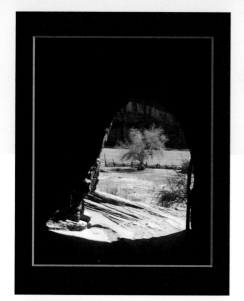

The center-weighted metering mode is useful for reading light on images like this one in which you want the priority given to the center of the image.

This scene was correctly metered using the manual metering mode to capture detail in the truck.

TIPS

Did You Know?

Many digital cameras have selectable auto-focus points that enable you to focus on off-center subjects. If your camera has this feature, check to see if one of your metering modes is linked to the selectable auto-focus points. This feature makes it easy to focus on an off-center subject, such as the tree photo that was shot from inside a cave shown in this task, and to meter the light from that same point.

Photo Tip!

When your chosen exposure-metering mode does not result in the exposure that you want, you have two choices. You can either adjust the exposure by using exposure compensation (see Task #25) or by using the manual mode, in which you choose both the aperture and shutter speed settings without any assistance from the built-in meter.

USING THE HISTOGRAM
to get the exposure that you want

One of the most useful features found on some, but not all, digital cameras is the histogram. The *histogram* is a graphical chart that shows the brightness levels of an image ranging from pure black on the left to pure white on the right, in 256 steps. The vertical scale shows how many pixels are found in the image at each brightness level.

Using the histogram, you can easily read the exposure of a photo. The more pixels there are to the right, the brighter the image is. Conversely, the more pixels there are to the left, the darker the

image is. The histogram also gives you a clear indication when you have *blown-out* highlights (see Task #26), which in most cases you want to avoid.

Although it is tempting to shoot to get a perfect histogram — that is, one nicely centered and dispersed across the full brightness range — such a histogram does not mean that it is a good exposure. The sample photos and histograms shown in this task illustrate the importance of getting the right histogram for the subject and your intended exposure.

The Canon PowerShot G2 digital camera shows a histogram along with a small thumbnail image and important camera settings on an LCD screen.

This pure white iris was correctly exposed using a built-in metering mode, a histogram, and exposure compensation.

This histogram of the white iris indicates a correctly exposed image, as the image is skewed to the bright side of the tonal range to keep the white iris white.

This nearly pure black Black Beauty iris was incorrectly exposed as a medium tone, which makes it appear purple rather than black.

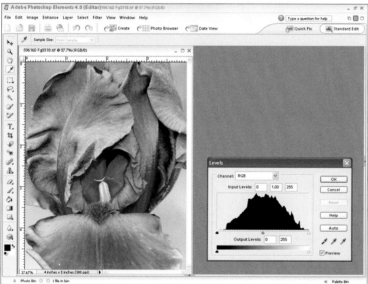

This histogram shows no black or near black tones in the very black Black Beauty iris. The exposure needs to be reduced.

TIPS

Caution!

Many digital cameras enable you to change the brightness of the LCD screen used to view images that you are about to take or have taken. Changing the brightness level or viewing the screen in bright light can cause you to misread the exposure. If your camera offers a histogram, you can use its graphical chart to give you an accurate view of the exposure, regardless of the LCD screen brightness setting or bright light.

Did You Know?

Digital photo editors, such as Adobe Photoshop Elements, have a feature that is similar to the histogram on some digital cameras for reading the overall brightness of an image. The Levels command provides a histogram along with the ability to modify the tonal range and overall image contrast.

Improve exposure with
EXPOSURE COMPENSATION

In some cases, the built-in light meter in your camera results in a bad exposure even if you choose a reasonable exposure mode (see Task #22) and the most appropriate metering mode (see Task #23). To get a good exposure, use exposure compensation if your camera offers that feature.

Exposure compensation enables you to modify the exposure up or down from the metered reading by a specified amount. By doing this, you can continue shooting using the modified meter reading settings and get good exposures. For example, if the meter reading indicates the need for a shutter speed of $\frac{1}{60}$ of a second at f/5.6, a +1 exposure compensation would modify the aperture setting to f/4.0 if the shutter priority mode was selected, or to $\frac{1}{30}$ of a second if the aperture priority mode was selected.

Using exposure compensation can be particularly useful when shooting in bright areas such as a beach, when snow fills most of the scene, or when shooting in a backlit situation in which light comes from behind the subject, leaving the subject in shadow and the background bright.

METERED SETTINGS

This photo was shot using the metered settings.

+1

This photo was shot with a +1 exposure compensation setting.

+1⅓

This photo was shot with a +1⅓ exposure compensation setting.

+2

This photo was shot with a +2 exposure compensation setting and is a good exposure.

Did You Know?

Using an exposure-compensation feature is the easy way to modify the built-in metering system to get the exposures that you want. If, for example, you are shooting a scene that is covered in snow, you can dial in the exposure compensation setting to adjust the built-in meter so that you get perfect photographs each time you press the shutter release.

Photo Tip!

There may be times when you want to shoot with more than a +2 or -2 exposure compensation. In those cases, you should choose the manual shooting mode. If the exposure compensation that you want is outside the range of your camera, you may need to change the ISO setting.

Avoid blown-out
HIGHLIGHTS

If any photography rule should not be broken, it is that you should avoid blown-out highlights, unless you want them for creative reasons. A *blown-out* highlight occurs when you use exposure settings that make part of the image pure white where there should be details.

The problem with pure white has to do with the mathematics behind digital images. Although you can usually bring out some detail in nearly black or shadow areas, you cannot bring out detail in areas that are pure white using a digital image editor such as Adobe Photoshop Elements.

If your camera LCD has a histogram, it likely also has a *highlight alert,* which is a feature that shows blinking bright white pixels on a thumbnail image. These blinking white pixels mean that you need to decrease the exposure until there are no more blown-out highlights. If a histogram shows a number of pixels at the extreme right, this is also an indication that you need to reduce your exposure.

This horse portrait has been overexposed. The pure white area on the face has no detail and cannot be brought back into the photo with an image editor.

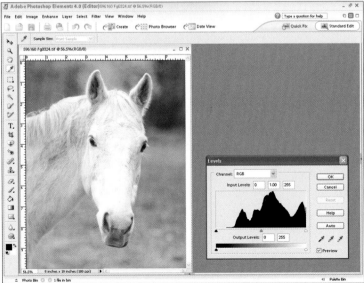

This histogram shows how much of the detail in the horse's face has been pushed into the no-detail highlight area.

The pure white spectral highlights or reflections on this well-exposed photo of the shiny steel headlight are correct.

DIFFICULTY LEVEL

The smooth white marble on the top of the head and on the arm of this statue should be nearly pure white because there is little detail to show.

 TIPS

Did You Know?

When shooting with a digital camera, you should usually use exposure settings to properly expose for the highlight area of a scene. Using an image editor such as Adobe Photoshop Elements, you can often bring details back into an underexposed area; you cannot, however, bring detail back from an overexposed highlight area where all the details are blown out because there are few or no details in the near white or pure white areas.

Did You Know?

One place that pure white is acceptable is where there are spectral highlights. A *spectral highlight is* a bright spot from a shiny highly reflective surface. Generally, spectral highlights should be small and very focused.

Understanding
DYNAMIC RANGE

Photography and print professionals refer to the range between the darkest parts of an image and the lightest parts of an image as the *dynamic range,* or *tonal range.* A composition that has very bright parts, such as a bright white sky, and very dark parts where there are deep shadows is said to have a wide dynamic range. Another commonly used term for such a scene is *high contrast.* Unfortunately, film or digital cameras are not able to capture detail in many wide dynamic range scenes.

The challenge that you face when shooting a high contrast scene is to capture details in the shadow areas *and* in the highlight areas. As new digital technologies are developed, there are a growing number of approaches that you can take (see Task #28). For example, you can shoot once to expose for the highlights and once to expose for the shadows and merge the two images together using an image editor such as Photoshop Elements. Or you can shoot once using the RAW format and convert the image twice — once for shadow detail and once for highlight detail. You then merge the two together.

This photo reveals detail in the white sign but not in the bird's dark feathers because the dynamic range is too wide.

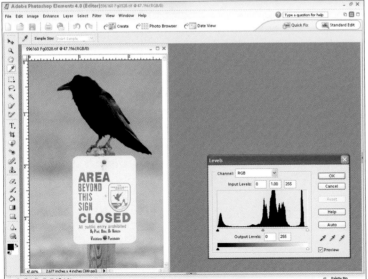

This histogram represents the tonal range of the preceding photo.

This is a classic example of the difficulty of getting details in a bright sky while showing details in a dark foreground.

DIFFICULTY LEVEL

Here detail is shown in the shadow areas, which causes a loss of detail in the sky.

TIPS

Did You Know?

Many film photographers use a graduated neutral density filter to enable them to capture a wide dynamic range. Although this filter, which gradually changes from dark to light in a vertical direction, helps to capture a wide dynamic range, it does so in a less realistic manner than you can do when combining two images with a digital photo editor (see Task #28).

Photo Tip!

You can expose a scene with a wide dynamic range to get excellent silhouettes (see Task #12). You can also shoot to capture detail in the shadow area of a landscape photo to make a bright white sky become a blown-out highlight. This makes it easy to replace the sky with a better sky found in another photo. To accomplish this task, you will need an image editor such as Photoshop Elements.

Combine two photos to get a
FULL DYNAMIC RANGE

One of the great things about digital photography is that there is virtually no limit to what you can do with one or more photos when you are skilled with an image editor. When you shoot a challenging composition that has a wide dynamic range, you can make an image that shows the full dynamic range in one of two ways.

First, you can shoot two separate photos — one exposed for the shadows and one for the highlights — and then combine them with an image editor. To get the photos to register exactly, you need to use a

tripod and to shoot without any moving objects in the scene.

Alternatively, you can take one photo using the RAW format and use a RAW converter such as Adobe Photoshop Camera RAW, which is included with Photoshop Elements, to convert the photo twice. First, convert it using an exposure setting to expose for the highlights and then convert it to expose for the shadows. Finally, use an image editor to combine them.

This photo was exposed to capture detail in the shadow area, or the foreground.

This photo was exposed to capture detail in the highlight area so that there is good detail in the clouds in the sky.

Combining the first two photos using an image editor shows the full dynamic range.

This photo was saved in the RAW format and later converted to expose detail in the shadow area, or the foreground.

This photo was saved in the RAW format and later converted to show good detail in the clouds in the sky.

The preceding two images were combined using an image editor to show the full dynamic range.

TIPS

Did You Know?

You may have a more visible dynamic range in your digital photos than you can see. A good-quality computer monitor that has been carefully calibrated to show a wide dynamic range is essential to seeing and properly editing digital photos. To calibrate your monitor, see Chapter 9.

Photo Tip!

In many cases, you will not be able to take two photographs set to different exposures so that they can be combined. Examples include scenes with moving subjects, such as fast-moving clouds or wildlife. In these cases, you can shoot using the RAW format and change the exposure using a converter.

Control Focus and Depth of Field

Incorrect focus control, limited depth of field, subject movement, and camera movement can all cause a blurry photo. Sometimes you may intend to blur a photo while other times it is an unwanted characteristic of a "not-quite-right" photo. To get the photos that you want, you need to be able to control focus and depth of field.

These two important photography variables affect each and every photo that you take. Although you need to understand how to control focus and depth of field and to understand the various tradeoffs you are faced with when making one decision over another, it is also equally important to be able to visualize the effect that you will get.

For example, you need to be able to have a good idea of how much depth of field you will have when shooting with a 100mm lens four feet away from the subject using an aperture setting of f/4 instead of f/8. The more you shoot and study your shots using the EXIF data, the better you will get at choosing your settings and setting up to get the photographs that you want. See Task #46 to learn more about EXIF data.

Focus and depth of field are two variables that enable a digital photographer to shoot more creatively. To develop the "mental view," shoot a few series of photos of various combinations of these variables and then study them carefully.

Top 100

ACHIEVE SHARP FOCUS #29
using a tripod

If you shoot in low light levels, use a slow shutter speed, or want to maximize depth of field by shooting with a small aperture, you will need to use a tripod to take sharply focused photos. The longer the focal length of lens you use, the more important it is to use a tripod because even the slightest movement can blur a photo. Besides enabling you to consistently take sharply focused photos, a tripod also makes it easy for you to shoot a more precisely and carefully composed photo.

Carrying and using a tripod can initially be bothersome. However, if you select a good tripod and head and you get used to using it and taking sharply focused photos, it will be hard for you to take photos without one. If you plan on shooting panoramas (see Task #52), consider getting a tripod head that has an independent panning feature such as the Manfrotto 488RC2 shown in this task. Photographers that regularly use a tripod get better photographs. If you are not using one, get one and use it.

DIFFICULTY LEVEL

A solid tripod such as the Manfrotto 3221WN is helpful for getting sharply focused and well-composed photos.

The Manfrotto 352 ball head is a lightweight, easy-to-use ball head.

The Manfrotto 488RC2 ball head has a separate lever and a graduated scale for panning. A quick-release lets you quickly and easily mount a camera on a tripod.

Control focus with
FOCUS POINT SELECTION #30

The shallower the depth of field, the more important it is to precisely select the part of the composition that you want clearly focused. If you are shooting a composition that has an off-center element that should be in focus, check your camera manual to learn about the features it has for selecting focus points.

There are three common types of features for selecting the focus area. Some cameras have a *fixed focus point,* usually in the center. With a *center focus point,* you aim that point on the subject where you

want critical focus, press the shutter button halfway to use automatic focus, recompose the picture, and then press the shutter button the rest of the way to take a picture. Some cameras enable you to select anywhere from 3 to as many as 50 focus points. After selecting the focus point, you simply compose and take the picture. Many cameras also have *automatic focus point selection,* which, surprisingly, often picks the best focus point for the subject.

An off-center focus point keeps the lady examining necklaces in focus.

Aiming the center focus point on the shack and locking focus keeps this red crab shack in focus.

The photo was then recomposed and the shutter release button pressed all the way down to capture the image.

SHOW ACTION
using a slow shutter speed

DIFFICULTY LEVEL

Usually, the objective is to use a shutter speed that is fast enough to stop any action in a photograph. However, you can use a slow enough shutter speed that your subject is partly blurred to show movement. To avoid getting a blurred background due to the slow shutter speed, use a tripod to limit the blur to the moving subject.

Choosing the right shutter speed is critical. Choosing one that is too slow yields too much blur. Choosing one that is too fast eliminates any sense of movement. With a little experimentation, you can learn which shutter speeds you need to get the results that you want.

If there is too much bright light, your camera may not have a small enough aperture setting to show motion. In such cases, you can either shoot when there is less bright light or use a neutral density filter to block some of the light entering the camera, which enables you to choose a slower shutter speed. To learn more about photographing with a neutral density filter, see Task #50.

This photo shows off the horses' magnificence because it was taken at ⅟₃₀th of a second to reveal the speed of their gallop.

The action in this photo of a boy jumping shows how much fun he was having and how much effort he expended.

In bright sunlight, even a very fast shutter speed can slow the propeller of an airplane taxiing on a runway.

ADD DRAMA
by panning with the subject

DIFFICULTY LEVEL

Another technique for showing action is to pan the camera with a horizontally moving subject. The result can be a dramatic photo showing the subject clearly focused against a nicely blurred background that is blurred horizontally.

The challenging parts of this technique are to choose the right shutter speed, pick the right background, and pan with the subject so that the moving subject is not blurred due to a panning speed that does not match the speed of the moving subject.

Getting the effect you want when panning with a camera requires considerable experimentation and

some skill, so you will need to practice. You must consider many variables, including the speed of the moving subject, the distance between you and the subject, the distance between the subject and the background, focal length, shutter speed, and the capabilities of your camera. Additionally, you need to be able to skillfully pan with the subject. Using a tripod head that has independent panning motion or a fluid head video camera tripod head can be useful for getting well-panned photographs.

A slow shutter speed of $\frac{1}{6}$th of a second caused the panning motion to blur the BMX riders to make an artsy print.

A shutter speed of $\frac{1}{125}$th of a second was used to freeze the flying pelican against the wonderfully colored and blurred background of a seaside harbor.

CONTROL FOCUS CREATIVELY
with manual focus

A flawlessly in-focus photo may not always be what you want. Imaginative photographers experiment with all the photography variables to get new and exciting photographs. Focus is one of those variables that you can change to dramatically alter a picture. A soft, out-of-focus photo can result in a mood that cannot be shown in a well-focused photo of the same subject. Likewise, you can carefully control focus to place emphasis on the subject or on an important part of a composition.

When you want to either take a picture that is out of focus or to have precise control over focus and where to position the depth of field, use a manual focus to get exactly what you want. Freeing yourself from one more automatic feature helps you to thoroughly think through another important aspect of your photography — focus. Try setting your camera to manual focus and use it to be more creative.

Manual focus made it easy to control precisely where the shallow depth of field was positioned on these soft-focused tulips.

Here, manual focus gave the photographer precise control over which part of the bee was in focus.

Getting the intended area of tulips in focus in this photo was easy with the camera set to manual focus.

 # 33

DIFFICULTY LEVEL

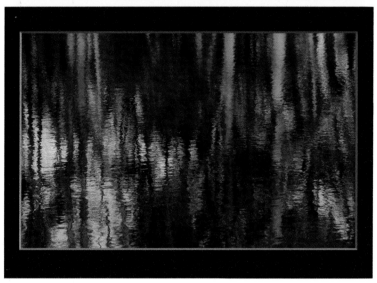

This intentionally out-of-focus photo of reflections in a pond was taken to be combined with another photograph using an image editor.

TIPS

Did You Know?

Some of the world's greatest photographs have been taken with cameras that were manually focused because automatically focusing cameras were not available. In those early days, professional photographers worked hard to refine their picture-taking skills, and their success remains as proof that you do not need an expensive, feature-rich camera to take great photographs.

Photo Tip!

Precise manual focus is difficult to get with many compact digital cameras. If you are having problems focusing in manual mode, consider getting a macro positioning rail such as the Manfrotto 3419 micro positioning plate. This tripod head accessory enables you to move your camera forward or backward using a dial to get perfect focus distance without having to move your tripod.

Control
DEPTH OF FIELD

Depth of field is the area in a photograph that is in focus. It is determined by three primary factors: the aperture setting, the distance to the subject, and the focal length. The smaller the aperture opening, the more depth of field you will have. For example, an f-stop of f/4.0 will be larger than an f-stop of f/8.0, and it will consequently have less depth of field. As the distance from the camera to the subject increases, so will the depth of field. Lenses with longer focal lengths have a shallower depth of field than lenses with short focal lengths. For example, a 100mm lens has considerably less depth of field than a 28mm lens.

Clearly understanding and being able to control depth of field is a significant part of photography. Besides using depth of field to isolate a subject from its background or to ensure that everything in the picture is sharply focused to show as much detail as is possible, there are many other creative uses as well.

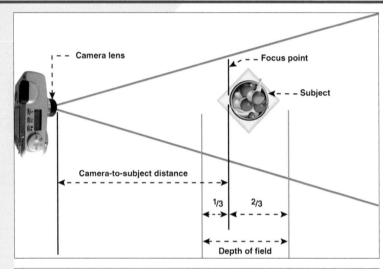

One-third of the depth of field is in front of the focus point, and two-thirds is behind the focus point.

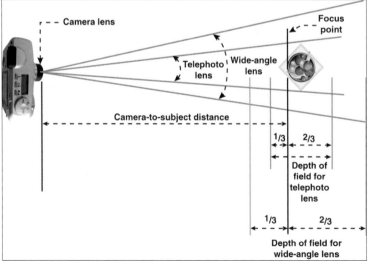

Shorter focal length lenses (such as 35mm) have more depth of field than long focal length lenses (such as 100mm) when the camera-to-subject distance is equal.

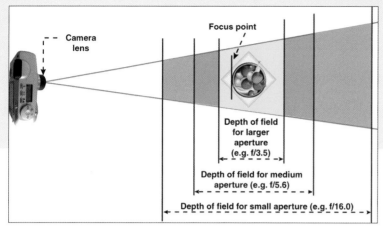

Aperture size is one determinant of depth of field. Small apertures result in greater depth of fields. A wide-angle lens has more depth of field than a telephoto lens.

DIFFICULTY LEVEL

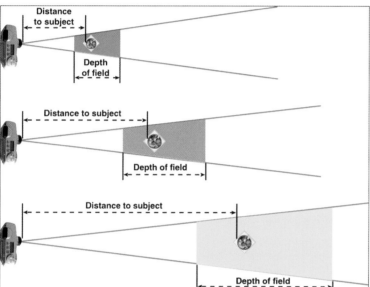

Camera-to-subject distance is one of three factors that affect depth of field. The farther away a subject is from the camera, the greater the depth of field will be.

TIPS

Did You Know?

The larger the aperture, the "faster" the lens is because it lets in more light than a slower lens or one with a smaller aperture – in the same amount of time.

Photo Tip!

When you want the maximum depth of field and you are shooting in low light, or you are shooting close-up or macro shots, the movement of the camera caused by pressing the shutter release button can cause unwanted image blur. To avoid camera movement caused by pressing the shutter button, set the timer release so that the camera takes a photo without your pressing the shutter release button.

CREATE COOL EFFECTS
with depth of field

Depth of field is determined by three factors: how close you are to the subject, what focal length lens you are using, and what aperture setting you are using. The farther away you are from the point where you set focus, the deeper the depth of field is. The longer the focal length you use, the shallower the depth of field is. The smaller the aperture you use, the more depth of field you have. You need to understand the relationships between all three of these factors to effectively control depth of field.

Photography is all about controlling a wide range of variables and understanding the tradeoffs when choosing settings. When you use a longer focal length lens to get a shallower depth of field, you will be able to show less of the subject due to a smaller angle of view. Using a smaller aperture to get more depth of field will require a longer exposure. Shooting farther away from the subject makes it harder to get a tightly cropped subject.

Using a lens with a long focal length and selecting a large aperture to get a shallow depth of field isolate these three flowers from the background.

A wide-angle lens with a small aperture was used to keep the entire archway photo in focus. A tripod was also used to minimize camera movement that would have blurred the shot with the required slow shutter speed.

A wide-angle lens with deep depth of field made it easy to keep all the pumpkins and the pumpkin stand in focus in this photo.

Depth of field is very shallow when shooting close up to a subject, such as this dragonfly, with a long telephoto lens and when using a mid-range aperture to minimize subject movement caused by wind.

TIPS

Did You Know?

Due to the small size of the image sensor used in many compact digital cameras, it is very hard to control depth of field because any of the available aperture settings produce a rather deep depth of field. If you mostly want to shoot photos with little blur due to a shallow depth of field, such a camera is wonderful. If instead, you want to be able to shoot subjects with blurred backgrounds, you may need to buy a digital SLR that enables you to shoot with a shallow depth of field.

Photo Tip!

When you are taking a portrait, try using a long focal length to get a small depth of field to focus attention on your subject and get a soft blurred background.

Understanding
FOCAL LENGTH

Technically, *focal length* is the distance in millimeters between the optical center of the lens and the image sensor in a digital camera when the lens is focused on infinity. However, focal length by itself does not describe the angle of view as is commonly thought. The angle of view is highly dependent on *both* the focal length and the size of the image sensor on which the lens focuses its image.

To make it easy to compare angles of view, the camera industry is fast accepting the term

"35mm equivalent focal length." Long focal-length lenses, such as a 200mm "35mm equivalent focal length," have a narrower angle of view than lenses with a shorter focal length such as 50mm. To capture a wider angle of view, you need a wide-angle lens. To get really wide-angle photographs, you can shoot multiple photos and digitally stitch them together; see Task #52 to shoot multiple photos to make a panorama.

FOCAL LENGTH MULTIPLIER
You can usually find the focal length multiplier for your camera in your camera's documentation.

NIKON COOLPIX 5700 ZOOM LENS
The Nikon CoolPix 5700 has a zoom lens with a focal length noted as 8.9mm to 71.2mm. The focal length multiplier is 3.93. The 35mm equivalent focal length is 35mm (3.93 x 8.9) to 280mm (3.93 x 71.2).

36

The photo on the left demonstrates the shortest focal length, 35mm.

The photo on the right shows an intermediate zoom.

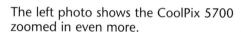
DIFFICULTY LEVEL

The left photo shows the CoolPix 5700 zoomed in even more.

The right photo shows the longest focal length of 280mm.

TIPS

Did You Know?

Many zoom cameras have an X rating, such as 2X or 4X, which is not directly related to the focal length. It just means that the maximum focal length is "X times" longer than the minimum focal length. For example, the Nikon CoolPix 5700 has an 8X zoom lens, which simply means that the longest focal length is 8 times longer than the shortest focal length.

Photo Tip!

Some digital cameras have a digital zoom feature that gives you an even longer focal length than you get with the optical zoom. *Optical zoom* is done solely through the optics of the lens. *Digital zoom* is actually the center of the composition enlarged digitally, and it is extremely inferior to optical zoom.

CONTROL PERSPECTIVE
with focal length

When you stand in the middle of railroad tracks that vanish into the horizon, you are experiencing *perspective.* When you experience perspective, straight lines seem to converge over distance. When shooting photos with a camera, you can use focal length to control how rapidly parallel lines converge or if they converge at all. The shorter the focal length, the more rapidly parallel lines converge.

To shoot a full-frame picture of a large building with a wide-angle lens, you have to be fairly close, and the building's lines will tend to converge over a short distance. If you shoot farther back from the building with a telephoto lens, you can still fill the frame, but you can do so without allowing perspective to make the building look distorted due to the rapidly converging lines that are really parallel lines.

Unfortunately, many of the zoom lenses on compact digital cameras suffer from barrel or pin-cushion distortion. These distortions are in addition to the convergence of parallel lines, and they result in lines that either curve in or curve out instead of remaining straight.

The façade of this office building shows severe convergence of parallel horizontal lines because it was taken up close with a wide-angle lens.

The white grid laid over this building shows the curving of building lines that should be straight. This distortion is caused by using a wide-angle lens.

This photo was taken with a wide-angle lens to include the house and a wide expanse of the sky and the tree.

#37

DIFFICULTY LEVEL

You can notice more perspective distortion of the house in this photo than the preceding one because the photo was taken close to the house.

Did You Know?

Several software applications are available to correct various types of image distortion, such as barrel and pin-cushion distortion, which are caused by wide-angle lenses. One product is LensDoc from Andromeda Software Inc. (www.andromeda.com). It offers specific corrections for many specific camera models, and Andromeda has versions for PC and Mac.

Did You Know?

You can use an image editor, such as Adobe Photoshop Elements, to correct the convergence of lines in a photo taken with a wide-angle lens. Select Image, Transform, and then Perspective to make lines that should be parallel actually parallel.

CONTROL BACKGROUND
with focal length and aperture

Controlling the background in a photo is often a key factor in getting a good composition. You can easily control the background with a long focal length lens, which has a shallow depth of field and a narrow angle of view. The shallow depth of field helps to create a soft-focused background. The narrow view makes it easier to change the background by moving the camera location to the left or right, or even up or down a few inches, with minimal effect on the composition of the subject.

Several factors determine how much you can control the background. The distance from the camera to the subject and the distance between the subject and the background are two important factors, along with the focal length. The closer the camera is to the subject, the narrower the depth of field will be, which helps to blur the background. Likewise, the farther the background is from the subject, the more you can blur the background. A tripod is a good aid to precise composition and successful control of the background when shooting with a long focal length lens.

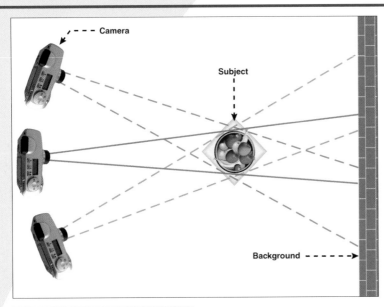

The longer the focal length of a lens, the more a slight move to the right or left may change the background.

The lady in this portrait was carefully positioned to make a nice soft background with colors that enhance the subject.

The softly blurred background with contrasting colors helps to isolate and focus attention on the flowers in the foreground.

38

DIFFICULTY LEVEL

The closer the background is to the subject, the more difficult it is to get a softly blurred background.

Did You Know?

Aperture settings are written as f/4.0 or f/8.0. But, in fact, the aperture size is really ¼.₀, or ¼, and ⅛.₀, or ⅛, which means that an f/4.0 aperture is actually larger than an f/8.0 aperture because one-fourth is larger than one-eighth.

Photo Tip!

The greatest depth of field is obtained by selecting the smallest aperture. When shooting with a small aperture, you need to use a slower shutter speed to get a proper exposure. This is why you need to use a tripod when the objective is to shoot with the maximum depth of field.

Chapter 5

Take Better Photos

Taking good photographs has more to do with a photographer's vision; the time she has to spend shooting, reviewing, and digitally editing her photos; and the knowledge of her camera than buying and using expensive photographic equipment. Undoubtedly, some of the more expensive digital cameras enable you to take better photographs, but if you really want to improve your photographic success, learn how to shoot better. Learn to choose subjects that you are passionate about. Assess and choose good shooting conditions. Determine your own photographic vision. Use your knowledge of your camera to capture that vision.

You also need lots of time to shoot, study, edit, and wait. You may need to wait for better light, less wind, or even for the subjects that you want to arrive. When conditions are good and you are ready to shoot, you must have your photographic vision, and you will need to know how to compose. The exciting new world of digital photography offers every photographer many new benefits that make it easier, faster, and cheaper to learn to make excellent photographs more often.

What makes good photos? One of the best standards to use to determine if you have taken a good photograph is to simply ask yourself if you like it and if you enjoyed the process of making it. Listen to the advice and opinions of others, but shoot for yourself and your own enjoyment. If you do, and you work hard and put in the time, you will become a good or maybe even a great photographer.

Top 100

Assess
SHOOTING CONDITIONS

For many reasons, you should make it a habit to carefully assess shooting conditions before taking any pictures. Besides determining if it is worth your time to shoot at all, you should also decide how to get the best photographs you can from the existing conditions. You may also consider when you may want to return to get better photographs.

What are good shooting conditions? Does wind, rain, snow, or bright midday sun make bad shooting conditions? One of the amazing things about photography is that there are few rules that always

hold true. Although it is safe to say that it is more difficult to get good photos with midday sun, you can find many remarkable examples of how wrong it is to always accept such a guideline as a rule.

Also consider the subject as one of the most important shooting conditions. If you are passionate about the subject, you will not only enjoy shooting more, but your results will ultimately be better. Having an interest in the subject and some knowledge about it can help you capture and portray its soul in an exciting or interesting way.

Would an early morning shot with light illuminating the white farm buildings improve this evening shot?

Is this a good beach color? Will it get better later? Should you use a faster shutter speed to underexpose it a bit for richer colors?

Could you choose a better background for this white poodle?

Is there too much wind to get a well-focused photo of this bee bathed in rich garden colors? Or does the wind help to create a soft-focus effect?

Can good photos be taken in a snowstorm? How will this scene look in an hour, two hours, or even more?

Photo Tip!

When you are shooting in less than ideal conditions, look for inventive ways to get good photographs. A torrential downpour may leave you with wonderful patterns in water puddles that reflect your subject. Or wind that is too fast to enable you to take close-up photos may help you get award-winning soft-focus photos if you use a slow shutter speed to capture blowing flowers.

Did You Know?

A surprising number of excellent photographs have been taken in "bad" weather. Heavy fog, thunderstorms, and snow blizzards often make for excellent photographs. The next time that you think the weather is bad, go shoot and see what you get. In particular, look for changes in weather.

Consider the
POSSIBILITIES

Each time that you press the shutter button to take a picture, you analyze dozens of different variables, including exposure, composition, lighting, depth of field, angle of view, and ISO setting. To get better photos, think about how you can change the variables to take many different photographs. Study them to find the ones that you like.

The more you experiment and study your results, the more likely you are to get an understanding of what you like and how to further develop your own personal style. For good practice, carefully consider

how you can shoot differently. Because many good photographers shoot the same subjects, getting fresh and interesting photographs that you will be proud of demands considerable thought.

When one of the world's most famous photographers was asked to review another photographer's portfolio, he looked quickly and said, "Take a couple of weeks and go shoot a few thousand more photos." He replied this way because the other photographer had not yet considered enough of the possibilities.

The exposure was increased slightly over the metered exposure to brighten the statue.

This exposure was the result of the camera's metering.

A slightly underexposed setting causes the background to disappear.

This slightly tighter framed photo puts more attention on the hand gesture.

This tightly cropped photo emphasizes the face.

40

DIFFICULTY LEVEL

This horizontal composition helps the viewer feel more "face to face" with the statue.

TIPS

Apply It!

You can sometimes get new and interesting photographs by going to extremes. Shoot at extreme f-stops, extreme shutter speeds, and extreme angles of view. Then, back off just a bit. Maybe try the other extreme and then back off just a bit. Ample experimentation will eventually yield photos that you like.

Photo Tip!

The most common view of a subject or scene is from a vantage point about five to six feet from the ground. Because most people view the world from this height, photos taken from this height are often ordinary. Try shooting from a worm's-eye or bird's-eye view to give viewers a fresh or unusual perspective.

COMPOSE
for maximum effect

How you compose is one of the most important decisions that you make about any photograph that you take. Although many guidelines help you to compose well, most of them have been routinely broken while still creating excellent photographs. So use the common rules, such as the "rule of thirds" (locate the main subject on one of the intersecting lines of an imaginary tic-tac-toe board overlaid on the image), as mere guidelines, not as hard-and-fast rules that cannot be broken.

Using a digital camera with a zoom lens enables you to try different compositions without having to move as much. You can shoot a wide-angle photo and then zoom in to compose a much tighter view of the subject. The angle of view and vantage points are two other significant aspects of composition that you can control somewhat when using a zoom lens. Look for creative angles that show your subject or scene in new and interesting ways. Also, look for ways to accentuate form, texture, and patterns. If you have composed a photo that invites the viewer to look more closely, most likely you have composed well.

This photo was composed using the "rule of thirds."

Framing the swamp with the foreground trees made this more interesting than an unframed version.

Adding a long expanse of the rusty hood in this photo shows where this dirty junkyard cat is napping in the sun.

A soft background keeps focus on the tiny green tree frog.

41

DIFFICULTY LEVEL

Composing the shot of this building in this way further emphasizes the architectural perspective.

TIPS

Apply It!

You can help convey information to the viewer about your subject by framing a photo with the foreground. Applying this powerful technique also makes viewers feel as if they are in the photo. Without this foreground, there is nothing but the subject.

Did You Know?

It takes effort to see new ways to compose. Yet, if you took a dozen good photographers and asked them to shoot the same subject, there would be many, many different compositions. Find a subject and see how many different compositions you can shoot as an exercise to further your composition skills.

Shoot photos based on a
THEME

For a number of good reasons, you should shoot photos based on a theme. First, if you have chosen a theme that you are interested in, you will enjoy taking the photographs for it, and capturing the theme can be a motivating factor to get you shooting. You will also find that you will become a better photographer as you continue to learn and work toward getting better and better photographs of a similar subject. Having more than one or just a few photos of a subject helps you to compare what is good and not so good in each shot that you take.

You can choose to shoot a theme that can be completed — for example, all the country churches in a specific county. Or you can choose a more open-ended theme such as antique automobiles, old barns, or even gargoyles. The photos in this task are good examples of one very specific theme — antique automobile hood ornaments. Notice that all but one of them are Mack truck hood ornaments. What theme should you pick?

This Mack truck hood ornament was shot to have a soft background.

The rust on this hood gives a clue to the age of the vehicle that the ornament is mounted on.

This is a hood ornament from a Mack fire truck.

This graceful hood ornament is from an antique Packard automobile.

Here is another Mack truck hood ornament shown against a rusted truck body.

Apply It!

As you shoot photos based on a theme, carefully consider how you compose them and how they will work together as a series. Should you shoot some in portrait mode and others in landscape mode? Should you attempt to have similar backgrounds, or can the backgrounds vary?

Did You Know?

If you have chosen a theme that requires considerable searching, use the Internet to get help shooting your theme. If you are a bird photographer, find a forum where other birders can tell you where to find certain birds. Or maybe you need help finding old barns. The Internet can save you considerable time and travel expense when searching for subjects that fit your theme.

Work to
DEVELOP YOUR STYLE

If you have seen a photograph and said, "That photograph had to have been taken by . . ." and you can correctly name the photographer, you have found a photographer who has a well-developed *style*. What makes a style? It can be the way a photographer portrays a subject, uses light, or captures colors. Or it may be a more difficult-to-quantify combination of characteristics that, when combined, make the style noteworthy.

How do you develop a style of your own? Take several photographs to develop your photographic vision and learn more about what it is you see and how you portray it. After you have taken thousands of photos, you will begin to see a pattern. Maybe you have an eye for shooting things that are graphic with bold colors, or you have worked on an impressionistic style by shooting in soft light on windy days with slow shutter speeds. When you notice a style developing, work on it to make it more distinctive, and keep refining it.

This purple and yellow iris is isolated from the soft green background with a telephoto lens.

The vantage point was chosen to provide a sharp contrast between the purple iris and the soft green background.

The aperture was chosen to keep this iris entirely in focus while allowing the background to be soft.

The distance from the iris to the background helped make a soft background for this sharply focused iris.

These two photos taken by Larry Berman (www.alternatephoto.com) show a style unique to Larry because of the color infrared technique he uses and the way he portrays ordinary subjects.

Part of Larry Berman's style involves choosing ordinary subjects but shooting them in extraordinary ways.

TIPS

Did You Know?

Many of the world's most successful and well-known photographers have a style that makes their work notable. Check out the works of Annie Leibowitz, Freeman Patterson, Pete Turner, and Jerry Uelsmann — to name just a few of the great ones.

Did You Know?

If you want to sell your photographs in an art show or display them in a gallery, you are more likely to have your work shown if you have a distinct style, shoot on a theme, or both. A series of random photographs with no connection can be considerably less interesting than a group of photos with a consistent style or theme.

SHOOT DETAILS
to create interest

Although the first and natural inclination is to shoot an entire subject, shooting tightly cropped details can lead to the creation of captivating photos. Detail photos often are more interesting than full-subject shots because you can take a photograph that shows either detail that the viewer had never noticed or detail that may cause the viewer to take a closer look while wondering what the subject is.

Capturing just part of a subject enables you to put emphasis on the detail that is ordinarily overlooked when viewing the entire subject. When composing detail photos, compose to show form, color, texture, or shape.

When shooting details, be aware of the fact that you can shoot an increasing level of detail, too. For example, you can shoot just part of a tree with an interesting shape, such as a specific branch, a few leaves, a single leaf, or even just part of a leaf showing the intricate lines and texture. As you get to increasingly smaller detail, you may want to consider using a macro lens or macro feature.

The close-up photo of this iris was taken to reveal details not ordinarily noticed in photographs that show the entire iris.

The intricate detail of decay in this ancient church alcove adds interest.

A tightly cropped photo of a custom motorcycle engine makes a wonderful print.

Here is a detail photo of the arched concrete support beams in a church walkway that connects two buildings.

This close-up shot of a sandhill crane reveals incredible detail, including a hole in its beak.

Apply It!

To catch a viewer's interest, take a photo of just part of a subject to let the viewer imagine what the rest of the subject looks like or to even make her wonder what it is that she is looking at. Also, detail-oriented photos can frequently reveal details to viewers that they would not normally have noticed.

Photo Tip!

When shooting a detailed photo with a small subject, use a macro lens or shoot in macro mode if one is available on your digital camera. Shooting with a shallow depth of field can often further add to the success of the photo.

Compose for final
PRINT PROPORTIONS

One challenge when photographing with a digital camera is to compose an image in the viewfinder that will translate into an image with the width-to-height proportions that you want. This problem arises because the aspect ratio of the image sensor is usually not the same aspect ratio as the paper you print on or the proportions of the image you want to put on a Web page.

Even though your images may be composed perfectly in the viewfinder, the viewfinder does not have the

same aspect ratio as many standard-sized prints, such as 4" x 6" or 8" x 10". This means that you have to crop the printed image. Think about how you will use your photos and shoot accordingly. To avoid having a less-than-perfect photo for any purpose, shoot more than one photo composed for each intended use. The owl photos in this task show how hard it is to get even one standard-sized print that looks good from a tightly framed original photo.

This original uncropped image fits well within the camera's viewfinder.

More space above the owl's head would be nice in this 11" x 14" print.

Similarly, more space above the owl's head would be nice in this 8" x 10" print.

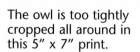

The owl is too tightly cropped all around in this 5" x 7" print.

This 4" x 6" print works well, unlike all the other standard sizes.

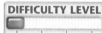
DIFFICULTY LEVEL

This 10" x 8" print shows the difficulty of printing horizontally if the photo was composed vertically.

TIPS

Caution!

If you are concerned about having to crop an image to get the width-to-height proportions for a print or an image for a Web page, make sure that you have set your camera to the largest resolution setting. If you use less than the maximum resolution, you may not have an image that is suitable for your intended use after it has been cropped.

Did You Know?

Using a digital image editor, such as Adobe Photoshop Elements, you can add some width or height to a photo if you are unable to crop it to the width-to-height proportions that you want. After adding some width or height to your image, use a cloning tool to paint in the extra needed width or height.

Learn to shoot better by studying
EXIF DATA

When you take a digital picture, the camera writes the image to an image file, along with other useful additional information such as the date and time that the picture was taken. The camera also records settings such as shutter speed, aperture, exposure compensation, program mode, ISO speed, metering mode, white balance setting, and flash information.

All this information is written to the image file in an industry standard format called the EXIF (exchangeable image file) format. To read this information, you need software that enables you to extract the EXIF data. Most digital camera

vendors provide image browser software that lets you read EXIF data while browsing thumbnail images. Also, you can read EXIF data from most image-management applications such as Cerious Software's ThumbsPlus (www.cerious.com) and ACD Systems's ACDSee (www.acdsystems.com). Adobe Photoshop Elements and Adobe Photoshop CS2 offer a file-browsing feature that you can use to view EXIF data. Additionally, some third-party vendors create free, specialized applications for reading and printing EXIF data, such as Thumber (www.tawbaware. com) and Exifer (www.exifer.friedemann.info).

Here is a digital photo with the camera settings stored according to the EXIF specifications.

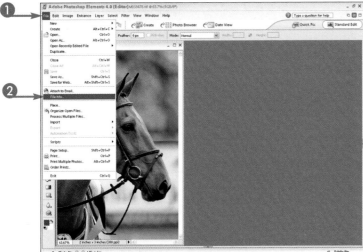

VIEW EXIF DATA IN PHOTOSHOP ELEMENTS EDITOR

1 With the file whose EXIF data you want to view open, click File.

2 Click File Info.

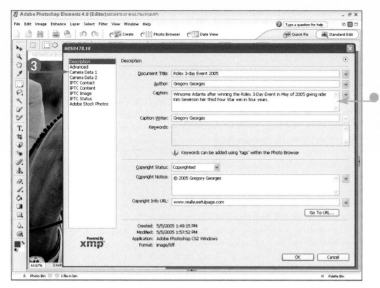

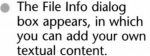

46

- The File Info dialog box appears, in which you can add your own textual content.

③ Click Camera Data 1.

The EXIF data appears, including the shutter speed, f-stop, ISO, and focal length settings.

④ Click OK when you are finished examining the EXIF data.

TIPS

Apply It!

EXIF data can be useful for learning how to take better photos. After taking a few photos with different f-stops to control the depth of field or when shooting multiple shots with different exposures using exposure compensation, look at the image and the EXIF data to learn which settings were the best.

Did You Know?

Besides being able to read the EXIF data that is written into a digital photo file by the camera, you can also add your own textual information. Open an image in Adobe Photoshop Elements Editor and click File ➪ File Info to open the File Info dialog box. Click any one of the IPTC links to show dialog boxes where you can enter image titles, copyright notices, keywords, and much more.

Get better photos with
PATIENCE, PRACTICE, AND EFFORT

Photography is an art. As is true with all art, the creation of good art takes patience, practice, and effort. Some amateur photographers buy expensive digital cameras and expect to immediately get wonderful photographs. After taking a few hundred photographs with minor success, they get discouraged and stop shooting. To prevent this from happening to you, use a good work ethic and patience to shoot lots of photographs, and you will see your efforts pay off.

Although a photographic vision of what you want to shoot and the ability to use your camera to capture that vision are essential to getting great shots, time spent shooting and patience to wait for the best shooting conditions significantly affect your photographic success.

Remember that when you shoot digitally, an important part of digital photography is editing with a digital photo editor such as Adobe Photoshop Elements. After you shoot, open your photos in an image editor and work as hard to learn how to edit your photos as you did to take them.

Take a hike to get you and your camera to new and exciting places to shoot.

Great photos often require extraordinary effort, such as getting into a pond with hip waders to get close-up shots of a water lily.

This photographer is patiently sitting while waiting for the perfect sunset at a well-chosen location.

47

Studying images and EXIF data on a computer will help this photographer improve his picture-taking skills.

TIPS

Did You Know?

Many professional photographers that shoot with film cameras shoot between 20 and 30 rolls of 36-exposure film per day, which is about 700 to 1,000 photos per day. With digital cameras, the cost to shoot each photo is less, and you have the advantage of instantly viewing the photo that you took.

Did You Know?

One of the best ways to learn more about photography is to shoot often and shoot several pictures of the same subject or scene using different camera settings and compositions. Then, study the results by viewing them along with the EXIF data on your computer screen. If you did not get it right, try again until you get the shot that you want.

Chapter 6

Try Creative Photo Techniques

Although you can take snapshots to document the events around you, the finer form of photography is all about having a vision of a photo that you want and then being able to use your camera to capture that vision. To develop your vision and increase your ability to effectively use your camera to capture it, you need to experiment and try different ideas. The more you shoot, experiment, and study your work and the work of others, the better your photography will be.

Coming up with creative photo ideas is easy, and you will often be pleased with your results. In addition to trying ideas that are presented in photography books, you should also think of new ideas yourself.

For example, you can experiment with different features on your camera and use them creatively. Push each of the available settings to the extreme to see what results you get. Maximum and minimum aperture settings and low shutter speeds are just two settings that can help you get exciting photographs. Also, you should think about how to make various design elements more pronounced. Think of ways to shoot that put focus on the subject, capture bold or subtle colors, or reveal patterns or shapes in complex scenes, or just shoot to capture elements or backgrounds to later combine with other images. The more you think how to shoot creatively, the more you will understand how to shoot well!

Top 100

FOCUS ATTENTION
on your subject

There are many ways that you can focus attention on your subject. Color, texture, background, focus, perspective, and a wide range of other visual design elements are just a few of the factors that you can use to draw attention toward your subject.

The next time that you shoot, think carefully about how you can focus more attention on the subject. Can you use a telephoto lens to fill the frame with the subject, or can you use a wide-angle lens to show a huge expanse of open space with a tiny subject that draws a viewer's attention? Maybe you can use a "new" vantage point where you look up at a subject that you ordinarily would look down at.

When using a long telephoto lens, you have considerable control over the depth of field, which enables you to show a sharply focused subject against a soft, blurred background with contrasting colors. Whatever strategy you use, placing more attention on your subject often results in a better photograph.

A long telephoto lens and a large aperture were used to make this purple iris stand out against a blurred background.

The bright green background of softly blurred plants helps focus attention on the spider on a web.

The camera was positioned a few inches up from the ground to focus attention on the boy's activity.

48

DIFFICULTY LEVEL

Part of a walkway attached to the building frames this high-rise office tower.

The face of this lacrosse player was shot to fill the frame to keep attention on his gaze toward the field.

TIPS

Photo Tip!

Use a telephoto lens when you want to isolate a subject from its background. Long focal length lenses have a shallow depth of field, and they therefore enable you to show a sharply focused subject against a soft out-of-focus background. When you want to isolate a subject with a telephoto lens, use a large aperture setting to keep your subject in focus while creating a soft background. See Tasks #34 to #38 for more about focal length and depth of field.

Photo Tip!

Sometimes the best way to focus attention on a subject is to keep your composition as simple as it can be. This strategy helps to minimize the number of distracting elements that may compete with the main subject.

Shoot color for
DRAMATIC PHOTOS

Color can be one of the most powerful elements in a photograph. Certain colors evoke emotions and create moods; others are less apt to be noticed. Red, for example, is always a color that is quickly noticed, even when it takes up a small part of a photo. Most scenes or subjects can become spectacular or relatively uninteresting depending on the color of the light that is available. Study colors to learn how they work together and how they can be combined to ruin a photo. Although heavily saturated bold colors can be dramatic, so can soft, subtle colors and even scenes with little color that result in a monochromatic photograph.

When you find a subject or scene that you like, visit and shoot it at different times of the day over a few days to see how different light changes the colors. Your repeated visits will help you learn how to capture color as you want it. Shooting subjects slightly out of focus and underexposing sometimes can further enhance your photos to produce rich, saturated color.

Richly saturated yellows, greens, and purples draw a viewer's attention to the iris.

The quality of the soft pastel colors along with the soft focus effect helps add interest to this water lily.

The contrasting bright red vine leaves make this mostly monochromatic bark texture more interesting.

The pink flowers in the background help to clearly delineate the edges of the white and blue iris in the center of this photo.

DIFFICULTY LEVEL

The awful combination of the olive green background against the purple and white iris shows how important it is to shoot to capture colors that work well together.

TIPS

Did You Know?

Color can sometimes say more in a photograph than the subject. Bold contrasting colors that are balanced on a page can give the viewer an entirely different impression than if the colors are not balanced and cause some tension.

Did You Know?

Some colors are more appealing than others. One of the reasons that the time just before and shortly after sunset is known as the "golden hour" is that the rich, warm, golden light bathes subjects in a very attractive rich, warm color. In contrast, colors in the blue family illuminate scenes in a cool color.

Show movement with a
NEUTRAL DENSITY FILTER

50

You can use a slow shutter speed to show movement by recording a moving subject as being partly blurred. However, sometimes you cannot choose a slow enough shutter speed when shooting in bright light because cameras have a limit to the minimum size of aperture opening. That limit may require a shutter speed that is too fast to show motion. In such cases, you can use a neutral density filter to reduce shutter speed by one or more stops.

A *neutral density filter* is nothing more than a glass lens filter that reduces the amount of light that gets to the image sensor in your digital camera without having any effect on color. Neutral density filters are usually rated as 2X, 4X, and 8X, and they decrease the light by 1, 2, and 3 stops, respectively. Generally, when you use a neutral density filter and a slow shutter speed to show motion, you will need to use a tripod.

To learn more about showing motion in your photos, see Tasks #31 and #32.

A combination of the shade from a tree and a neutral density filter allows a slow shutter speed to capture the motion of this person walking and gives her a ghost-like appearance.

Without the use of a neutral density filter, this photo of a motorcycle could not have been taken because there was too much light to use a slow enough shutter speed to create this panning effect.

Control reflection with a
POLARIZER

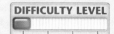
DIFFICULTY LEVEL

A *polarizer* is a filter that attaches to your lens. Polarizers have two primary uses: to remove light reflections and to enhance or deepen the color saturation. When you use a polarizer to increase the color saturation, you must shoot at a right angle to the sun. As you turn more toward or away from a right angle to the sun, you are able to control less of the effect. *Circular* polarizers can be rotated, which enables you to control the level of the effect. When you use a polarizer to enhance colors, you need to be careful to not overuse the effect, as it can result in a contrasty and wholly unacceptable photo.

When you want to shoot without the distraction from light reflections, you can use a polarizer to reduce or eliminate them altogether. A polarizer is useful, for example, when you want to shoot through a glass window and show what is on the other side or to shoot toward water and show what is beneath the surface. You can also use a polarizer to control bright reflections from reflective or shiny surfaces such as metal or glass.

Reflections of saturated colors of the trees and sky make the bottom of this shallow stream hard to see.

A polarizer filter removed the reflections so that the bottom of the stream is now visible.

Shoot photos for a
PANORAMA

As long as photographs have been taken, it has always been a challenge for photographers to capture the beauty found in wide-sweeping scenes. A wide-angle lens can capture more of a scene than a shorter focal length lens, but wide-angle lenses tend to add unwanted distortion to the photos, and they still do not capture as much of a scene as you often want. Using one of the digital stitching applications or a feature such as Adobe Photoshop Elements Photomerge, you can shoot and later combine multiple photos into a single, long vertical or horizontal panoramic photo.

When you shoot photos that you will later combine using a digital stitching application, you need to overlap each photo by ⅓ to ½ so that you can match and blend the images seamlessly. You also need to be careful to maintain the same exposure throughout your photos. Avoid shooting moving subjects such as clouds or ocean waves that make photos too different to be combined. Finally, you should always use a tripod.

These four photographs of a country landscape were taken with a camera mounted on a tripod with a head that allows panning.

This photo was created by digitally stitching together the four photos shown on the prior page. Adobe Photoshop Elements was used to stitch the images together and to make additional edits such as the color change.

DIFFICULTY LEVEL

 TIPS

Did You Know?
You can use the Adobe Photoshop Elements Photomerge feature to combine multiple photos into a single, large photo for making large prints. If your digital camera does not have enough pixels to make a quality print in the size that you want, you can shoot several photos and combine them with Photomerge.

Did You Know?
You can take multiple photos of vertical subjects and create vertical panoramas as easily as you can create horizontal panoramas. Good subjects for vertical panoramas include tall trees and buildings. Shooting from a distance with a telephoto lens can help minimize unwanted perspective distortion caused by using a lens with a shorter focal length.

Shoot photos with a "WOW!" FACTOR

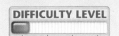
No matter what subjects you like to shoot, there are times where you can capture a photo with a "Wow!" factor. If you shoot sports photos, it may be a photo of two soccer players up in the air heading a ball at the same time, showing the intensity of the play with sweat flying off their faces as you capture the perfect moment when the ball is compressed between their heads.

Nature photographers are always looking to photograph elk with record-setting antlers, or the perfect red fox in golden light, or maybe a black bear mother with four cubs (a rare occurrence). To get photographs with a "Wow!" factor, you need to look for exceptional light, perfect natural specimens, or unusual occurrences, or maybe you just get enough of the photographic variables correct that you get an outstanding photograph through good vision, camera settings, and composition. Often the trick to getting a photo with a high "Wow!" factor is being in the right place at the right time and then using your skills to capture the perfect shot.

A row of black-necked stilts fishing together as a team is as amazing to watch as it is to see in a photo.

Wow! What is this foot attached to? Sometimes it is what is not in a photo that makes it interesting.

Thousands of wintering birds flying and grazing in open fields can be an awesome thing to see, hear, and photograph.

Shoot scenes with
LOW CONTRAST

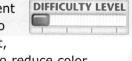

Soft, diffused light tends to reduce contrast and can be used to produce wonderful photographs. Unlike bright light that can create more contrast than you can capture on an image sensor (or film), soft light enables you to show good detail in all parts of an image, and it enables you to get excellent smooth gradations that can make superb photographs.

Learn to look for low-contrast light and take advantage of it when you find it. Early-morning or late-evening light is usually a good time to find low-contrast light with good color. Mist, fog, haze, or clouds can also create excellent low-contrast light that is a joy to shoot. Besides reducing contrast, these lighting conditions can also reduce color saturation and enable you to capture monochromatic images that can be simple and powerful.

Finding low-contrast light is not always easy. Some geographic areas rarely have anything but brightly lit skies, and other places are known for rarely having direct sunlight. Being able to shoot in low-contrast light is often a matter of place, time, and chance.

Heavy cloud cover and dense fog reduced the contrast in this photo taken in Ireland.

Low light levels help create the smooth two-toned gradation that is the background for this digitally edited tree.

The low-contrast light that creates the wonderful two-toned gradation enhances this simple photograph of a coastal waterway.

Shoot when
SEASONS CHANGE

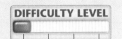

You can usually get out-of-the-ordinary photos by shooting when the seasons change. In early spring, you can find new buds that can be fascinating to watch as they open. Spring can also bring a nice contrast between the dark browns of winter plants and the green colors of the new spring plants.

Undoubtedly, the rich bold colors of fall can also be a key factor for getting extraordinary photos that are hard to match when shooting at any other time of the year. Determining the exact time to get the best

fall colors and when various plants and trees bloom is more a matter of chance than planning. The best approach for deciding when to go to shoot fall colors is to watch them yourself or find someone who can give you a daily update if you live too far away to visit except when shooting. These wonderful and rather short periods between seasons can provide you with some of the best photographic opportunities of the year.

Careful observation of nature in early spring can provide you with a deeper understanding of your subjects.

When a sweet gum tree grows new buds, it also hangs inedible spiny fruits for a few weeks before dropping them.

The opening of buds on many plants and trees can be amazing to watch and photograph over a few days.

Shoot
PATTERNS AND SHAPES

As a photographer, you can choose from many elements to draw attention to your photographs. Patterns and shapes can often become the strongest elements in a photograph, and you can find them everywhere after you develop a skill for noticing them and capturing them with your camera.

Our minds are always working to make sense of what our eyes see by looking for patterns and shapes in the complex and often over-cluttered environment that we live in. The result is that patterns and shapes are pleasing. Patterns are formed by the repetition of objects, shapes, lines, or colors. Sometimes it is the pattern or shape that makes a photograph a good one, rather than the subject itself. In fact, many good photographs feature a strong pattern or shape that is made by something that is not even recognizable.

When you find a pattern or shape, think how you should shoot it to make an interesting photograph. Use light to make a silhouette, or maybe even use bright highlights to strengthen the pattern or shape.

The softly focused lupine flowers in the background mirror the graceful shape of the blue lupine flower in the foreground.

This single elegant yellow fern's shape is enhanced by the shapes and orientation of the blurred grasses in the background.

The shape and color of this brightly colored wildflower add interest to this photograph.

SHOOT WITH A PLAN
to edit digitally

After you start taking photos with a digital camera and editing them with an image editor, you have moved into an entirely new world of possibilities. Each time that you shoot, you should be thinking about what it is you can or cannot do with your image editor after you have taken the photograph; otherwise, you will be vastly limiting what you can create photographically.

Because you can combine one or more photos or parts of photos, remove unwanted parts, substantially modify contrast and tonal range,

and much more, you need to think carefully about what you decide to shoot, how you shoot, and even what you may not want to shoot. In the past, because of the cost of film, you may have avoided taking a landscape photo that featured a telephone line or maybe a car that ruined the photo. Or maybe you avoided taking a photo because the contrast was too extreme. When you shoot and edit digitally, you can frequently correct these problems with an image editor.

This photo of a field of wildflowers was intentionally blurred so that it could be combined with the following photo to get a soft-focus, double-exposure effect.

This photo was taken to add to the preceding photo as a layer with a blend mode in an image editor.

Digital brush strokes and filter effects transformed this photo of the Sedona desert into a digital painting.

57

DIFFICULTY LEVEL

A pelican was shot specifically to become an object to use in another photo, such as this one of a swing in the woods.

An overexposed and slightly blurred photo was used to make this architectural image.

TIPS

Photo Tip!

Think about and shoot photo objects and backgrounds. The next time that you find a wonderful subject, such as an old car sitting in a field with an ugly bright sky, think "photo object." Then, when you find a perfect background scene for that car, shoot it and combine it with the old car and foreground.

Did You Know?

You should *always* work to take the best photo that you can when shooting. Many photographers new to digital photo editing believe that they can fix anything wrong with a photo after they have taken it. That is not always the case. You will always end up with a better photo after editing it, if you first start with an excellent photo.

Experiment to create
UNIQUE PHOTOS

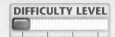
DIFFICULTY LEVEL

Break all the photography rules and guidelines that you know. Shoot with a slow shutter speed without a tripod. Zoom or pan your lens with the shutter open while shooting with a slow shutter speed. Intentionally overexpose and underexpose, shoot in high-contrast light, shoot in low light, shoot in the rain or a snow storm. Shoot a subject that you ordinarily do not shoot. Take 50 photos while shooting from ground level. Take 50 photos with your camera set to the smallest aperture. Shoot using extremes — extreme vantage points, extreme focal lengths, extreme aperture settings, and extreme distances to the subject.

When you shoot a popularly photographed subject or scene, think carefully about all the obvious and common shots that are taken and then try to come up with a dozen new ways to shoot the same subject or scene. Maybe you change the angle of view or the vantage point. Or shoot with a different light, or shoot from a distance and frame the subject with some foreground element. Experimentation and careful thinking about each photograph that you take are always good.

A slow shutter speed was used to create this photo of a BMX racer.

Attention is drawn to this statue by zooming the lens during exposure with a slow shutter speed.

Slight horizontal panning during exposure created this blurred sunset effect.

Shoot in low light for
RICH COLORS

#59

DIFFICULTY LEVEL

Long exposures in low-light environments can create rich, glowing colors that can make spectacular photographs. City streets at night, building interiors, or nighttime reflections in windows can be good subjects to shoot. Fairgrounds with brightly lit moving rides can result in some spectacular images with the brightly colored lights represented as blurred streaks of heavily saturated colors.

When you shoot in low-light levels, you need to use a tripod to get sharply focused photographs. To minimize camera shake caused by pressing the camera's shutter release and to further reduce any blur caused by camera movement, you can use a timed shutter release feature if your camera has one.

Richly colored sunsets can provide wonderful light for taking photos with dramatic color. Instead of shooting toward the sunset, turn and shoot away from the sunset using the light coming from the sun to light subjects of interest to you. Or you can use the light from brightly colored sunsets as backlight to get fantastic silhouettes with glowing backgrounds that outline the silhouetted subjects.

The vase of flowers shown through this archway is illuminated in rich colors that were captured in low light with a camera mounted on a tripod.

These church organ pipes were hardly noticeable in the low light level, but they glowed in a photo taken with a camera mounted on a tripod using a long exposure.

The richly saturated colors of this Las Vegas hotel were captured using an exposure time of two seconds.

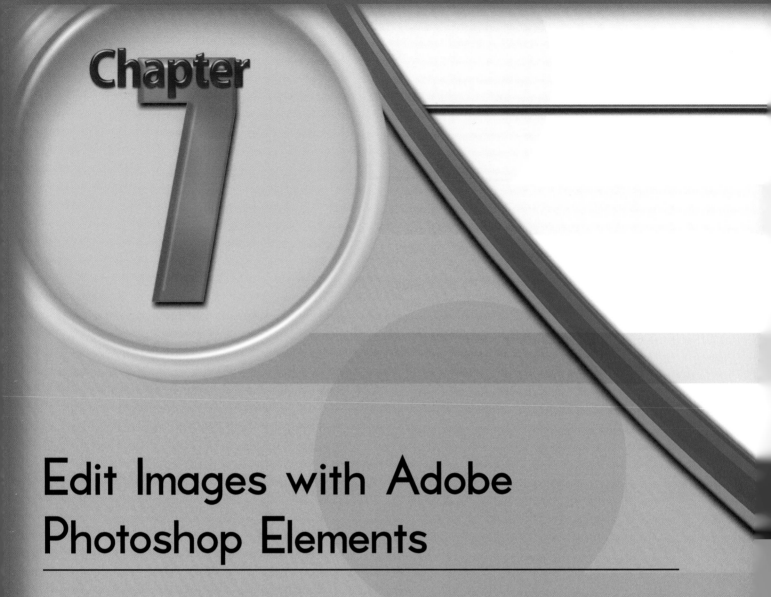

Chapter 7

Edit Images with Adobe Photoshop Elements

After you have taken photos with your digital camera and have downloaded them to your computer, they are ready to be digitally edited. Using an image editor such as Adobe Photoshop Elements, you can substantially improve the quality of an image, plus transform or alter your digital photos in an almost infinite number of ways. This chapter requires familiarity with basic Elements commands; to learn these commands or refresh your memory of them, see *Teach Yourself VISUALLY Photoshop Elements* (Wiley, 2005).

The first thing you should do before performing any edits is to evaluate each photo and make a plan. Consider a few important questions: Do the photos first need to be converted from the RAW format? How can you improve your digital photos in terms of color

and overall tonal range and contrast? How else do you want to alter or fix the photos? Do you need to add or remove elements? How will you be using the edited images? Will they be used on a Web page, shared as an attachment to an e-mail, or made into large prints on an inkjet printer?

Only after you have answered these questions will you be able to effectively edit your photos to get the results you want. The order of the steps that you take to edit your images is important. However, if you use features such as Undo History and adjustment layers, you will be able to go back to early steps and change settings or delete the steps entirely and start from that point on. It is also important that you learn when to save your image files to preserve your work and the quality of the image.

Top 100

Learn the best
EDITING SEQUENCE

The order of the steps that you take to edit your digital photos matters. Anytime you perform edits on a digital photo, you alter some of the original picture data. Although the image may look better, you have less original picture information than you did when you first opened the image. So the first step to take when editing an image is to save it under another filename so that you preserve the original "digital negative."

As you make various kinds of edits, you may find that you want to go back a few steps or change some of the settings used on an earlier step. You can do this without degrading image quality if you use Undo History and adjustment layers. Also, you want to make sure to perform any steps for increasing image size or sharpening at the end, *after* you have already saved your file.

Proper image-editing workflow may result in many copies of each image in addition to the never-edited original and an archived backup copy of important originals and edited versions.

1 Straighten, crop, adjust tonal range and contrast, and remove unwanted color casts.

2 Perform any additional image edits as needed except for image resizing or sharpening.

③ Save the image under a different filename than the original image.

● Optionally, you can save the file as a PSD file to preserve any layers.

④ Click Save.

DIFFICULTY LEVEL

⑤ Increase or decrease image size and sharpen the image for the target printer or to display onscreen.

⑥ Save the file as a flattened image if you plan to print the image in this size again.

Did You Know?

No matter how you increase the size of a digital photo, the image quality decreases to some extent. Because of this, you should generally complete your edits on the original-sized image and only increase image size when you know the specifications of the print size and the target printer.

Did You Know?

The best image-sharpening settings to use when applying the Adobe Photoshop Elements Unsharp Mask filter are very dependent on the size of the image and how you are going to use it. For this reason, you should apply the Unsharp Mask filter only when you know how you are going to use the image and what size you need.

Convert RAW files with
ADOBE CAMERA RAW

You realize some of the most significant benefits of using a digital camera only if you shoot in the RAW format. When you use the RAW format, you save your image without applying many of the camera's settings, such as white balance. Not only does this mean that you no longer have to worry about using some of the wrong camera settings, but you also have considerable control over how your picture looks *after* you take it.

Because RAW files are proprietary to each camera vendor, there are differences between vendors and

even specific camera models. You need to use a RAW image converter that supports your camera model to get an image that you can edit. Before purchasing the Adobe Camera RAW plug-in or any other RAW image file converter, make sure that the software supports your camera model.

After you install the Adobe Camera RAW plug-in, you can double-click RAW images in the Adobe Photoshop Elements file browser to open them in the Adobe Camera RAW dialog box and convert them. To learn more about the RAW file format, see Task #4.

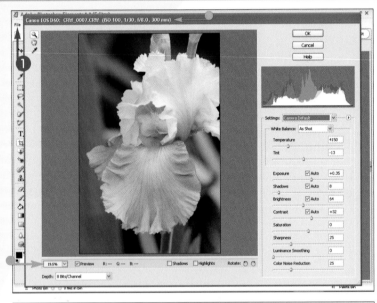

① In Elements, click File ➪ Open.

② Double-click the RAW file that you want to convert.

● The Adobe Camera RAW plug-in dialog box appears, listing the camera, filename, and EXIF information in the title bar.

● These options control the image preview.

③ Click here and select the appropriate shooting conditions for the picture.

The photo in this example contains too much blue, giving the flower an unnatural purple appearance.

● Alternatively, you can fine-tune white balance by dragging the Temperature and Tint sliders.

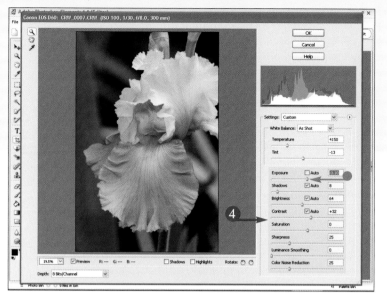

④ Adjust other settings as needed.

This photo was overexposed and required a decreased Exposure value.

● The Exposure slider enables you to adjust exposure compensation or tonal adjustments without compressing the image or losing any of the original image data.

DIFFICULTY LEVEL

⑤ Click here and select 8 or 16 Bits/Channel.

⑥ Click OK to apply your changes and close the dialog box.

Adobe Camera RAW saves the image in its current folder.

TIPS

Did You Know?

Camera vendors who sell digital cameras that support the RAW image format provide their own proprietary RAW image file converter software. However, generally the converters that are included with the camera are remarkably inferior to those provided by third-party vendors. The most popular RAW converters are Adobe's Camera RAW plug-in (www.adobe.com), Breeze Systems's BreezeBrowser (www.breezesys.com), and Bibble Labs's Bibble (www.bibblelabs.com).

Did You Know?

One disadvantage of using the RAW format is that it takes considerable computer processing power and time to convert RAW images. Also, you cannot view your RAW images as thumbnails in your thumbnail browser unless your camera's RAW files are supported.

Process a
BATCH OF PHOTOS

One of the most time-saving features in Adobe Photoshop Elements is the Process Multiple Files feature. This feature enables you to select a group of digital photos and perform a set of specified editing steps on them — and then write them all to a target destination folder.

This customizable automated process can be set up to rename files, resize images (see Task #70), convert file formats, perform basic image corrections,

and write captions or watermarks directly on the images. Although you will want to manually edit many of your photographs, you are likely to find times when you will find it extremely useful to save time and have the automated process correct your images quickly in a batch. The results you get will be similar to those that you get at a one-hour processing lab.

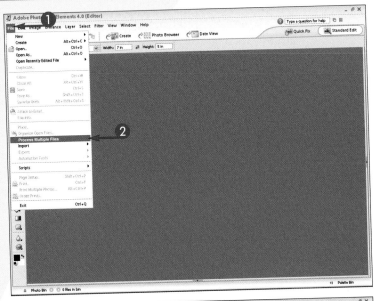

① In Photoshop Elements Editor, click File.

② Click Process Multiple Files.

The Process Multiple Files dialog box appears.

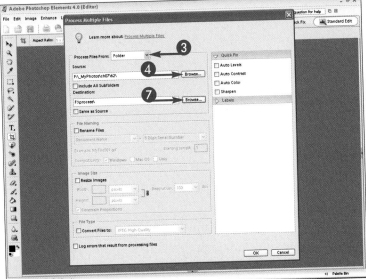

③ Click here and select Folder.

Note: You can also choose to use opened files or import from a camera.

④ Click Browse to select the source folder.

The Browse for Folder dialog box appears.

⑤ Click the folder that you want.

⑥ Click OK.

⑦ Back in the Process Multiple Files dialog box, click Browse and specify a destination folder.

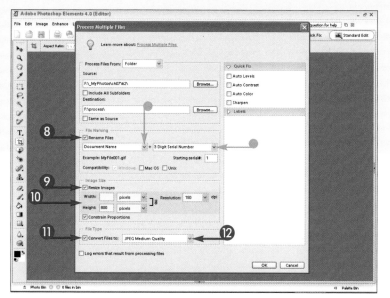

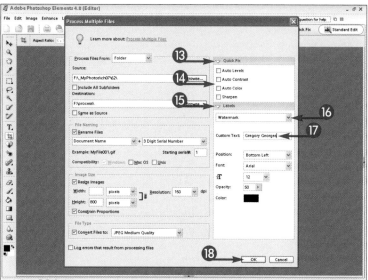

8 Click to check the Rename Files box if you want to rename the files.

● You can click here and select how the files are renamed.

9 Click to check the Resize Images box to resize the images.

10 Type in the width, height, and resolution.

11 Click to check the Convert Files To box to change the file format.

12 Click here and specify the file format.

13 Click here to show the editing options.

14 Click to check the boxes of the editing options that you want.

15 Click here to display the labeling options.

16 Click here and select Watermark or Caption.

17 Type any custom text that you want for the caption or watermark.

18 Click OK.

The batch of photos are processed and placed in the specified destination folder.

Did You Know?

You can easily add captions directly to your digital photos when using the Process Multiple Files feature if you have a description in the EXIF data (see Task #46). To add a caption to a digital photo file, click File ➪ File Info, type the caption in the Caption field, and then click OK to save the file. When using Process Multiple Files, you can turn on the Description feature and specify where the text should be placed and how it should look.

Caution!

When using the Process Multiple Files feature, you should be very careful not to use settings that overwrite your original files — thus ruining your originals forever. Be especially careful what destination folder you choose if you are writing captions or watermarks over your images.

Using the Clone Stamp tool to
REMOVE UNWANTED ELEMENTS

You can remove a variety of unwanted elements from your photos using a few different tools found in Adobe Photoshop Elements. You can remove everything from unwanted telephone lines or vehicles in landscape photos to people or objects in group photos. Without question, some elements are easier to remove than others. Most often, the best approach is to replace the unwanted element with another part of the image. If this is possible, the quickest approach is to use the Clone Stamp tool to "clone" existing areas over the unwanted elements.

The Clone Stamp tool enables you to set a *source point* in the image you are editing, or even another image. After you set the source point, you can paint with the Clone Stamp tool to replace the unwanted element with the image from the source.

You can also cut and paste one part of an image into another part to cover unwanted elements if the source image fits in terms of texture, color, or subject.

① Use the Zoom tool or the Navigator palette to zoom in on the area that you want to cover.

Note: Make sure to keep the area that you will use as the source area visible.

② Click the Clone Stamp tool.

③ Click here and select an appropriately sized soft-edge brush.

④ Click here and select Normal.

⑤ Click here and select 100%.

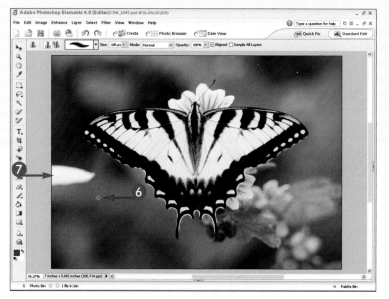

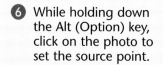

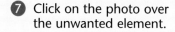

6 While holding down the Alt (Option) key, click on the photo to set the source point.

7 Click on the photo over the unwanted element.

Note: Multiple clicks are usually better than clicking and dragging.

DIFFICULTY LEVEL

The Clone Stamp tool paints over the unwanted element.

Note: Click often while painting so that you can easily remove any unwanted brush strokes with Ctrl+Z (⌘+Z).

Note: For better results, you can change the source point as needed.

Did You Know?

When you have a limited source area that can be used to replace an unwanted element, you can try adjusting the opacity to add some variation to the area you are painting. Then you can use the newly created area to use as a source for the remaining area that needs to be replaced.

Did You Know?

You can also use the Clone Stamp tool to add another element to an image. For example, if you take a family portrait that is missing one or more people, you can paint in the missing people by setting the source point to the people you need from another photograph.

Edit a
SELECTED AREA

Sometimes you may want to perform *selective edits,* which occur when you apply a filter or make edits to only a portion of the image instead of the entire image. To perform a selective edit, you must first select the area that you want to edit. Adobe Photoshop Elements offers many different tools for selecting parts of an image. Depending on the characteristics of the area that you want to select, one tool may be more appropriate than another. Or you may want to use more than one tool and keep adding to a selected area until you have selected all of the area that you want.

Good tools for selecting parts of an image include the Rectangular and Elliptical Marquee tools, the Lasso tool, the Magic Wand tool, and the Selection Brush tool. Some of these tools enable you to select parts of an image at a time and keep adding to the selection. Some tools, such as the Rectangular and Elliptical tools, also enable you to subtract from the selection by changing the selection mode in the Tool options bar.

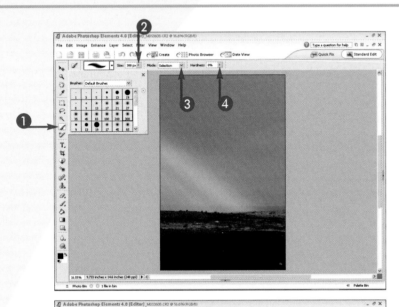

① Click the Selection Brush tool.

② Click here and select a brush size.

③ Click here and select Selection.

④ Click here and select 100%.

⑤ Use the Zoom tool to zoom in on the edge of the area that you want to select.

⑥ Using the Selection Brush tool, click and paint along the edge to select it.

A dotted line appears, showing your selection.

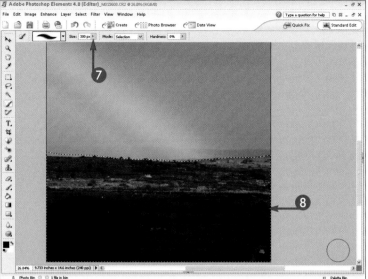

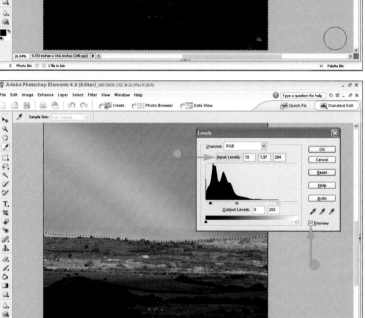

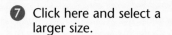

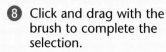

7 Click here and select a larger size.

8 Click and drag with the brush to complete the selection.

9 Make any changes that you want.

Note: Any edits that you make will be limited to just the selected area.

● In this example, the Levels command was applied to just the field in the foreground.

● Checking the Preview check box displays your edits in the document window.

Did You Know?

One of the challenges in selecting complex areas to edit independently of the rest of the images is to not lose your selection. If you think you may need to perform additional editing on a selected area, you can copy and paste it into the image as a new layer. However, if you do this, you will not be able to make global edits to the entire image unless you flatten the layers.

Did You Know?

When making selections with the Selection Brush tool, you should click and paint in small strokes, which enables you to step back one stroke using Ctrl+Z (⌘+Z) when you paint outside the intended area, thereby saving you from having to redo the entire selection.

KEEP TRACK
of your edits

Editing digital images is often a process of trial and error. You make a few edits and then decide if you like the results. If you do not like the results, the Undo History palette makes it easy to back up one or more steps. The Undo History palette keeps track of each step, which is called a *history state.* When you exceed the maximum number of history states set in Preferences, Elements deletes the earliest history state each time that you add a new one.

Using the Undo History palette, you can back up one or more steps and then move forward again by clicking each step in the palette while comparing the results. When you back up one or more steps and then make a new edit, however, Elements discards all steps from that point on as you add each new edit to the palette. You can also delete a history state by clicking it in the Undo History palette and then dragging it onto the Trash button at the bottom of the palette.

① Click Window.

② Click Undo History.

The Undo History palette appears.

● As you perform edits, Elements creates a history state in the Undo History palette for each edit.

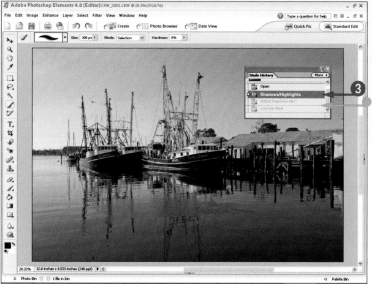

③ Click the history state at which you want to view the image.

● History states occurring after that time are "ghosted."

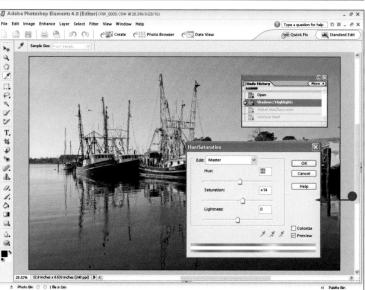

If you want to edit from that point on, perform the next edit, and the Undo History palette will reflect the new edit history.

● In this example, the Hue/Saturation command was applied using different settings.

TIPS

Did You Know?

When working on a large image, it can take considerable memory to maintain a long list of history states in the Undo History palette. You can increase or decrease the amount of Undo History states that are saved by changing the value in the History States box in the General Preferences dialog box. The default value is 50.

Did You Know?

You can back up one or more states in the Undo History palette without using the palette by simply pressing Ctrl+Z (⌘+Z), which is the shortcut keystroke for Step Backwards. If you want to go all the way back in history to the initial state, you can do so by clicking File ⇨ Revert.

USING ADJUSTMENT LAYERS
to gain editing flexibility

Whenever you apply the Levels, Brightness/Contrast, Hue/Saturation, Gradient Map, Invert, Threshold, or Posterize command, you make permanent changes to the image. You cannot go back and make minor adjustments to the settings of any one of these commands unless you step all the way back in the editing process using the Undo History palette. Then, if you change settings, you will lose all the steps following that step. However, if you use an adjustment layer when you apply any of these seven commands, you can always return to that layer and

make changes to the settings. This is such a powerful feature that it is usually wise to use adjustment layers when you apply any of these seven filters.

To create an adjustment layer, you select Layer ➪ New Adjustment Layer, and then pick one of the seven different types of adjustment layers to suit your needs. After creating a new layer, you can name it, and the adjustment layer shows up in the Layers palette.

See Task #65 to learn more about tracking your edits using the Undo History palette.

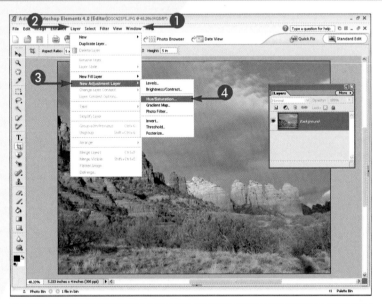

① Click Window ➪ Layers if the Layers palette is not showing.

② Click Layer.

③ Click New Adjustment Layer.

④ Click the type of adjustment layer that you want to create.

Note: For example, you click Hue/Saturation to create a Hue/Saturation adjustment layer.

The selected command's dialog box appears.

⑤ Specify the settings that you want.

⑥ Click OK to apply the settings.

You can add one or more adjustment layers or one or more edit steps.

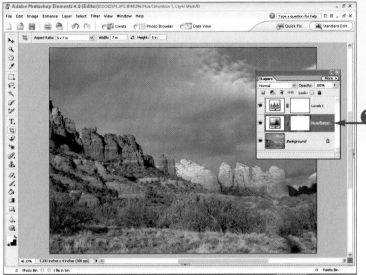

7 To modify previous settings, double-click the adjustment layer thumbnail.

The dialog box for the type of adjustment layer appears.

8 Make any adjustments to the initial settings that you want.

9 Click OK.

Elements applies the new settings to the adjustment layer.

TIPS

Did You Know?

You can turn on, or turn off, the effects of one or more adjustment layers by clicking the Layer Visibility icon (the eye) at the far left of each adjustment layer in the Layers palette.

Did You Know?

When you are sure that you will not need to make any further changes to an adjustment layer, you can flatten your image to reduce its file size. Click the layer that you no longer need to make it the active layer. Then click the More button in the upper-right corner of the Layers palette to get a pop-up menu. Click Merge Down to flatten one layer or click Flatten Image to flatten all the layers in the Layers palette.

Create a
PANORAMA

As long as photographs have been taken, it has been a challenge for photographers to capture the beauty found in wide-sweeping outdoor scenes. Wide-angle lenses can capture more of a scene than shorter focal length lenses, but wide-angle lenses tend to add unwanted distortion to the photos, and they still do not capture as much of a scene as is often wanted. Using one of the "digital stitching" applications or a feature such as Adobe Photoshop

Elements Photomerge, you can shoot and later combine multiple photos into a single long vertical or horizontal panoramic photo.

Task #52 shows how to take photographs that you can later digitally stitch into one panoramic print. If you have taken your own pictures for such a purpose, you are ready to use the Photomerge command in Adobe Photoshop Elements to do the stitching.

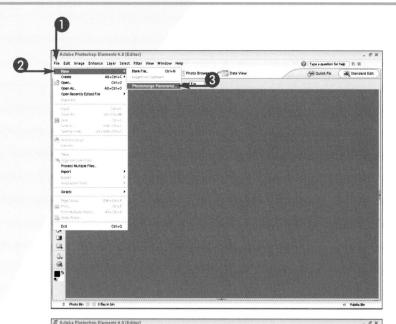

① Click File.

② Click New.

③ Click Photomerge Panorama.

The Photomerge dialog box appears.

④ Click Browse.

The Open dialog box appears.

⑤ Find and select the folder that contains the images you want to combine.

⑥ Press Ctrl and click each file to select it.

⑦ Click OK to close the Open dialog box.

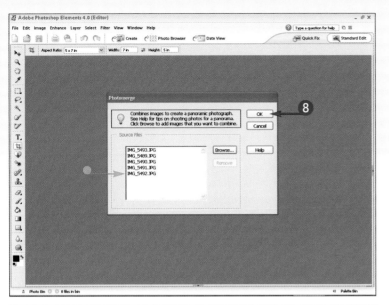

- The selected files appear here.

8 Click OK to add the files.

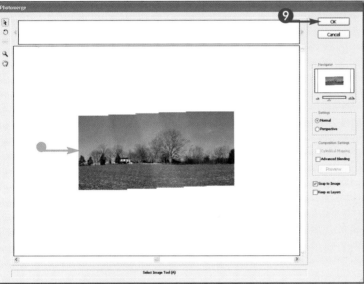

9 Click OK.

- Photomerge automatically stitches the images together.

Photo Tip!

You can use the Adobe Photoshop Elements Photomerge feature to combine multiple photos into a single large photo for making large prints. If your digital camera does not have enough pixels to make a quality print in the size that you want, you can shoot several photos and combine them with Photomerge.

Did You Know?

You can take multiple photos of vertical subjects and create vertical panoramas as easily as you can create horizontal panoramas. Good subjects for vertical panoramas include tall trees and buildings. Shooting from a distance with a telephoto lens helps minimize unwanted perspective distortion caused by using shorter focal length lenses.

Create a
PANORAMA

On rare occasions, Photomerge will not be able to automatically align your digital photos. When that occurs, you will see the photos placed in a window at the top of the Photomerge dialog box. To align the images, simply drag and place the images that were not automatically aligned. When you get the images close to where they should be, Photomerge should be able to automatically and precisely position them.

If you want to create more perspective than is visible in the combined images, you can select the

Perspective radio button and then click once in the image to select the vanishing point. Photomerge adds some perspective to the combined image. If you use the Perspective feature, it is important to have up to a 50 percent overlap in the photos that you are using; otherwise, gaps may occur between each image at the top and bottom of the combined images. Placing a check mark in the Advanced Blending box results in a more seamless blend between each image.

⑩ Click the Zoom tool to enlarge the panorama to fill the preview box.

⑪ Click Normal.

⑫ Click to place a check mark in the Advanced Blending box.

⑬ Click Preview to preview the merge.

⑭ After examining the preview, click Exit Preview.

⑮ Click OK.

Photomerge begins the merge process.

The merged image opens in a new document window.

⑯ Select the Crop tool to crop the image.

#67 CONTINUED

TIPS

Did You Know?

Some digital photo-stitching applications enable you to shoot a series of pictures that covers a full 360-degree view. You can then combine these images into a video that you can move to the left and right by clicking the image and dragging in the direction you want it to move. The view you get is similar to one where you stand in a single spot and turn around in a full circle looking out toward the horizon.

Did You Know?

Many digital cameras come with a variety of software applications including digital photo-stitching applications. Check any CD-ROMs and written documentation that came with your camera to see if you have one.

HAND-COLOR
black-and-white photos

One fun and easy traditional photo technique you can do digitally is to create a hand-colored black-and-white photo. The traditional approach requires that you paint on a photographic print with special photographic paints that take time to dry and are easily smeared. Plus, you have brushes and mixing palettes to clean up. Painting digitally is easy and fun, and the results can look wonderful if you take your time to select the right colors and paint carefully. Using a pen tablet such as those made by Wacom makes this technique much more successful than if you use a mouse to paint.

The most effective way to create a hand-colored black-and-white photo effect is to create one layer for each color that you use. Not only does this enable you to independently adjust each color with the Layer Opacity setting, but it also enables you to easily correct any mistakes. Additionally, you can apply Hue/Saturation changes to each color to get the perfect colors. If you want to build up each color gradually, you can vary the Opacity setting of the Brush tool.

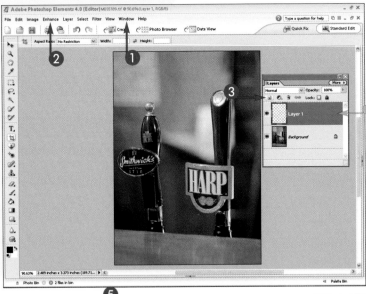

❶ Click Window ➪ Layers if the Layers palette is not showing.

❷ Click Enhance ➪ Adjust Color ➪ Remove Color to desaturate the image.

❸ Click the Create New Layer icon in the Layers palette to create a new layer for the first color.

● The layer appears in the Layers palette.

❹ Click the Brush tool.

❺ Click here and select an appropriate brush size.

❻ Click here and select Normal.

❼ Click here and select 100%.

DIFFICULTY LEVEL

8 Click here and select Color.

9 Click in the Foreground Color box to display the Color Picker.

10 Click the color that you want.

11 Click OK.

The Color Picker closes.

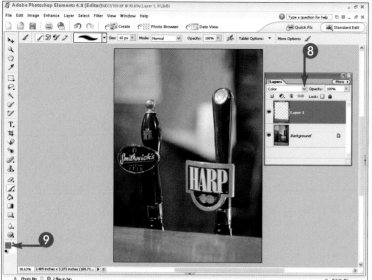

12 Click the image to begin painting.

13 Click here and select a lower Opacity value to tone down the color.

14 Continue to paint by choosing different colors and selecting appropriate brush sizes until painting is complete.

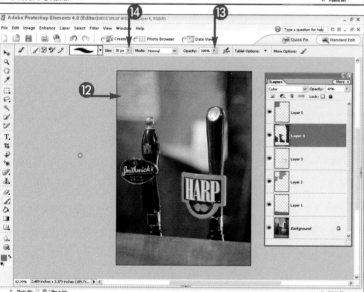

Did You Know?

An easy way to make a wonderful hand-colored black-and-white photo is to open a color photo and make a second copy. Convert one copy to a black-and-white photo and use the second copy as a color reference guide. You can use the Eyedropper tool to pick a color to use as the paint color for the black-and-white image. Remember to make one layer for each different color so that everything is reversible and changeable!

Did You Know?

Most beginners that try the hand-colored black-and-white photo technique use colors that are way too saturated and bold. Traditional hand-colored black-and-white photos are painted with subtle colors, and usually only a few colors are used.

PROTECT AND PRESERVE
original photo files

Saving a digital photo file is not all that hard. The hard part, if there is one, is learning when to save it. One of the most common mistakes made by those new to digital photography is to save a digital photo file over the original file after making edits to it with an image editor. When you do this, you no longer have an original image file, which can later prove to be a horrible loss. Even though you think that you have made the photo look better, over time your skills and knowledge of digital photo editing will improve, and you will wish you had the original file.

Never overwrite your original image files; they have the most "picture information" you will ever have. Most editing sessions deteriorate the image even if they do look better, so you should always protect your original digital photo files.

RENAME YOUR PROJECT

- After opening an original digital photo, you should save it to another folder, save it under a different name, or save it as a different file type to avoid overwriting the original file.

SAVE PROJECTS OFTEN

- Anytime that you have spent more than 30 minutes or so editing a file, you may want to consider saving the file using a suffix with one or two digits to indicate progressive edits.

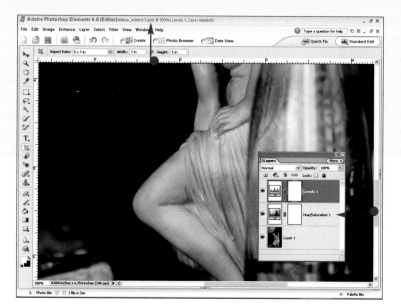

DIFFICULTY LEVEL

● Anytime that you use adjustment layers to add additional elements to your image, you should save the file as a PSD file so that you can access your layers later.

Note: If you save your image to a file format such as JPEG, you will never be able to access the separate layers again.

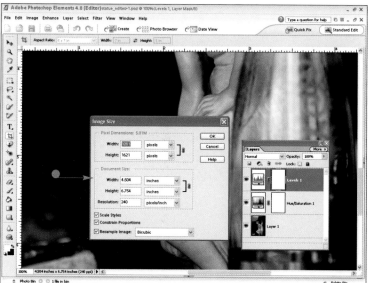

SAVE BEFORE SHARPENING AND RESIZING

After you have completed all your edits and before you have increased the size of the image or sharpened it, you should save the file.

● Sharpen an image and change its size only to output the image to a specific printer and display size.

TIPS

Caution!

A common mistake is to make edits to an image and then increase the image size and sharpen it, before the image is saved. Anytime that an image is increased in size, there will be some degradation in image quality. If you do not save your image after your edits are complete and before you have increased the image size, you will be saving a less-than-perfect image without any chance of going back.

Did You Know?

You can make a digital photo appear to be sharper using the Adobe Photoshop Elements Unsharp Mask command. This filter should only be applied to an image when there is no possibility that you will change the image size. The optimal settings for the Unsharp Mask are highly resolution dependent.

RESIZE A BATCH
of digital photos

When you want to convert a batch of digital photo files to the same file format or to the same size and resolution, you can easily do so with the Adobe Photoshop Elements Process Multiple Files feature. You simply need to put all the digital photo files that you want to convert, resize, and rename in one folder or a folder and subfolders. Then specify how you want to convert the images and which folder to use for the output folder.

You can also use the Adobe Photoshop Elements Process Multiple Files feature to automatically

rename a folder, or a folder and subfolders, of image files without making any changes to the files other than name changes (see Task #62). Just make sure to set the Convert Files To option to the type of files that you want to rename and to uncheck the Resize Images box.

This is a useful feature for rapidly and easily converting an entire folder of digital photos to use in a slideshow application, on a Web page, or for writing to a CD-ROM to have prints made at a digital photo-printing service company.

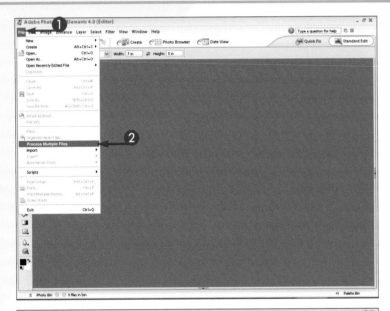

① Click File.

② Click Process Multiple Files.

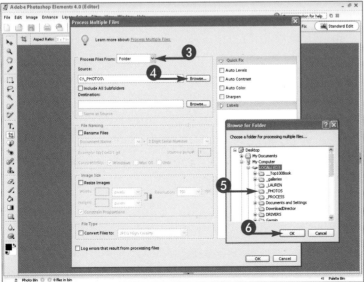

The Process Multiple Files dialog box appears.

③ Click here and select Folder.

④ Click Browse.

The Browse for Folder dialog box appears.

⑤ Click the source folder to select it.

⑥ Click OK.

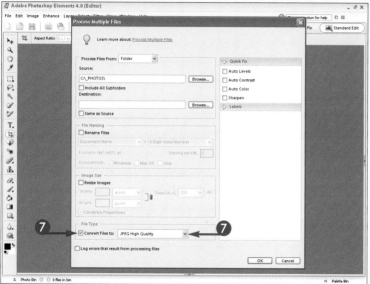

7 In the Process Multiple Files dialog box, click to check the Convert Files To box and select the output file type that you want.

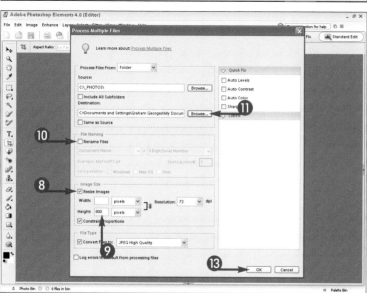

8 Click to check the Resize Images box.

9 Type in the image height that you want.

10 Uncheck the Rename Files box unless you want to rename the files.

11 Click Browse and select the destination folder in the Browse for Folder dialog box.

12 Click OK to close the Browse for Folder dialog box.

13 Click OK to begin the batch conversion.

Did You Know?

When you have a folder of images that you want to convert and resize so that the longest side is equal to a specified length, the Adobe Photoshop Elements Process Multiple Files command cannot be used when some of the images are taller than they are wide and others are wider than they are tall. To work around this problem, create two folders and put all the vertical images in one folder and the horizontal photos in the other folder. Then run the Process Multiple Files command on each folder using the same destination folder.

Edit photos for use on the
WEB

You can use the Adobe Photoshop Elements Save for Web command to convert your digital photos into images that are perfectly sized and suited to use on a Web page or as an e-mail attachment. Although it is possible to use the Save As command, the Save for Web command has many advantages.

Anytime that you save digital photos for use on a Web page, you are faced with a tradeoff between image file size and image quality. The more that you compress an image and the smaller the dimensions

of the image, the faster it downloads and displays, yet the more an image is compressed, the more the image quality is reduced. The Save For Web dialog box enables you to view the original along with the compressed image side-by-side for comparison. This enables you to select the file type and the level of compression to optimize the tradeoff between file size and image quality — the goal being the smallest file size with an acceptable image quality.

❶ Click File.

❷ Click Save for Web.

The Save For Web dialog box appears.

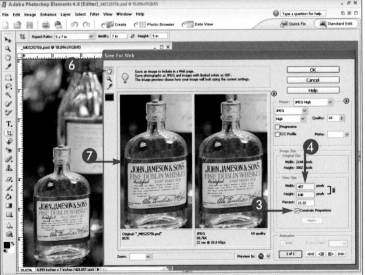

❸ Click to check the Constrain Proportions box.

❹ Type in either the width or height.

Elements sets the other dimension for you to keep the aspect ratio the same as the original.

❺ Click Apply to resize the file.

❻ Click the Hand tool.

❼ Click the image on the left and drag on it to view an area with detail.

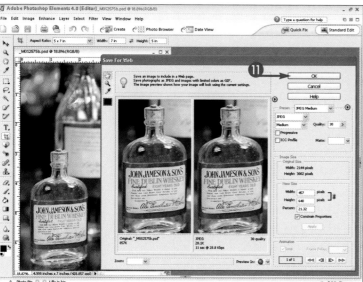

8 Click here and select JPEG Medium.

Note: JPEGs are compressed images that are small and useful for displaying on Web pages.

● In this example, the size of the image on the right is now 28.1KB instead of 857KB.

9 Click Quality and lower the setting until you get an unacceptable image quality.

10 Move the quality setting back up until you have acceptable quality.

11 Click OK.

The Save Optimized As dialog box appears, in which you can choose a folder and filename for the saved file.

12 Click Save.

The image is saved, optimized for the Web.

Did You Know?

The Adobe Photoshop Elements Save For Web dialog box offers an animation feature. To create animations, you need to add each image that you want to animate as a layer in a single image file. To view the animation, you click the Play button at the bottom of the dialog box. You can even set the animation to loop and set the frame delay time interval.

Did You Know?

You can fine-tune compression levels with the Quality slider found in the Adobe Photoshop Elements Save For Web dialog box. In addition to using the presets, you can set Quality from 0 to 100.

Chapter 8

Adjust Tonal Range and Correct Color with Photoshop Elements

The vast majority of problems from which digital photographs suffer fall into two categories: tonal range and color. Such interrelated problems include not having enough contrast, having too little detail in either the shadow areas or the highlight areas, dull colors, or colors that are simply not correct. Whether the problems result from bad lighting, incorrect camera settings, or poor exposure, you can often improve your images with Photoshop Elements.

Photoshop Elements offers an array of features that you can use to adjust your digital images. By far, the most popular tool for making corrections is Levels. Levels enables you to fine-tune the dark, midtone, and light pixels in an image and view the results immediately. You can use the Levels dialog box to fix both tonal range and color problems.

You can also apply a variety of specific filters to lighten, darken, and blend layers in an image. You can apply lighting commands such as Shadows/Highlights or use layer blend modes such as Multiply or Screen to improve the appearance of a photo.

When deciding how to fix a tonal range or color problem, start by duplicating the Background layer. Adding layers enables you to experiment with various features and editing techniques without making permanent changes to the original image. You can even use adjustment layers that will enable you to go back and make adjustments to settings you made earlier in the editing process without suffering any image degradation.

Top 100

CHECK EXPOSURE
with the histogram

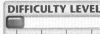

Before you begin making edits, you should first examine your photo carefully and determine an overall editing strategy. One of the first things to check is the tonal range using Levels.

The Levels dialog box gives you a good graphical representation, called a *histogram,* of how well or how poorly your image was exposed. The histogram plots out the light and dark pixels in an image in terms of their brightness level. It also shows you how much contrast the image has, displaying how

many pixels are in each of 256 tonal ranges. The more intense the grouping of pixels in an image, the taller the histogram reading for that particular tonal area of the image. For example, a histogram showing a large reading of dark pixels may need adjustments in tone or contrast to correct the image.

As you examine the histogram shown in the Levels dialog box, be aware that there is no such thing as a perfect histogram.

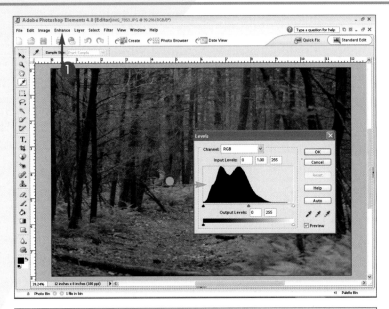

VIEW RGB LEVELS

① Click Enhance.

② Click Adjust Lighting.

③ Click Levels.

The Levels dialog box opens and displays the tonal range for all three RGB channels by default.

● This histogram indicates that the image is dark without pure blacks and without any light tones.

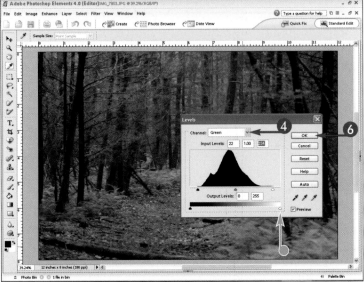

VIEW A COLOR LEVEL

④ Click here and select a color channel.

The Levels dialog box displays the selected channel tonal range.

⑤ Note approximately where the main tonal range begins and ends.

● You can adjust the tonal range by dragging the tonal markers for each color channel.

⑥ Click OK.

Elements applies your changes.

CHECK FOR COLOR CASTS
with the Info palette

Photoshop Elements includes a handy tool called the Info palette that you can use to evaluate the color values in a digital image. The Info palette enables you to check different pixels in an image to compare Red, Green, and Blue channel values. One of the best uses of this tool is to compare the color casts of two photos, such as an edited photo and an original photo. For example, you may check how your edits affect skin tone color from one photo to the other, or

you may check how much of a color boost occurs in a particular area of the photo after applying a filter.

As you move the mouse pointer over an image, the Info palette displays the numeric values for colors that appear beneath the pointer at any given spot on the photo. By default, the Info palette uses RGB mode to read a photo. You can also view Grayscale, Web, and HSB color values.

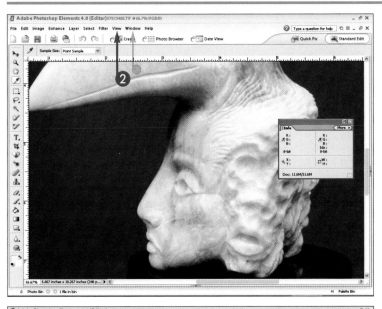

1 Display the Info palette.

● You can display the Info palette by clicking Window ➪ Info.

2 Click View ➪ Actual Pixels to zoom to 100%.

3 Click the Hand tool and move the image to where you can see an area that should be white or neutral gray.

4 Click the Eyedropper tool and move the mouse pointer over the image where you want it white or gray.

5 Read the RGB values in the Info palette.

This image has a blue cast because the Blue value is much higher (242) than the Red (234) or Green (237) values.

Fix
UNDER- AND OVEREXPOSED PHOTOS

One of the most common problems with photos is that they are either underexposed or overexposed. Although this is often a subjective determination, you can quickly lighten or darken an image by tinkering with a few of the layer blending modes available in Photoshop Elements. Blending modes enable you to change the way pixels mix between two layers of an image. For example, the Screen blending mode, when applied to an underexposed photo, always makes the image colors appear lighter. The Screen blending mode examines each channel's

color and multiplies the inverse of the blend layer and the base layer.

The Multiply blending mode makes the image colors darken, which is ideal for overexposed photos. The Multiply blending mode examines each channel's color values and multiplies the base color by the blend layer color. You also use the Multiply blending mode to intensify image colors.

With either blending mode, you can fine-tune the exposure lighting by adjusting the layer's Opacity setting.

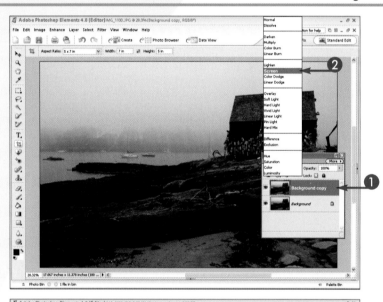

ADJUST UNDEREXPOSURE

This photo of a seaside building appears a bit underexposed.

① Create a copy of the Background layer in the Layers palette.

Note: You can create a quick layer copy by selecting Layer ⇨ Duplicate Layer and clicking OK.

② Click here and select the Screen mode.

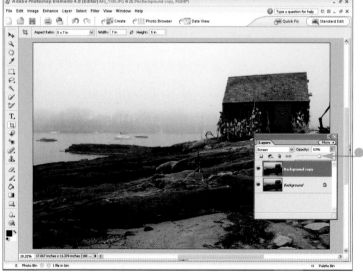

Elements immediately lightens the image.

● To make the blending effect more subtle, click and drag the Opacity slider to adjust exposure brightness.

Elements reduces the underexposure by lightening the image.

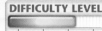

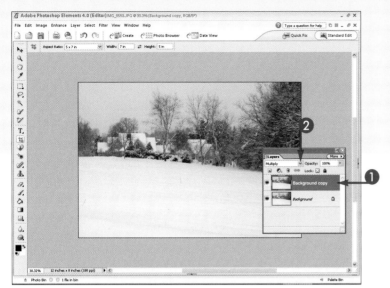

This photo of a snowscape appears a bit overexposed.

1 Create a copy of the Background layer.

Note: *You can create a quick layer copy by selecting Layer ⇨ Duplicate Layer and clicking OK.*

2 Click here and select the Multiply mode.

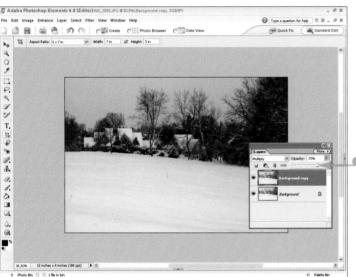

Elements immediately darkens the image.

● To make the blending effect more subtle, you can click and drag the Opacity slider to adjust the exposure brightness.

Elements reduces the overexposure by darkening the snowscape.

TIP

Did You Know?

Although you may be tempted to apply the Brightness and Contrast feature in Elements to correct exposure and contrast problems, this feature does not correct overly light or dark images. Instead, it either raises the brightness values in an image to make all the pixels brighter or lowers the values to make all the pixels darker. For most photos, you do not need to adjust all the pixels, just the ones affected by the exposure problem. For best results, use the blending modes and adjustment layers to correct exposure problems.

Understanding
CONTRAST

A good technique for improving many digital photographs is to look for ways to enhance the contrast in the images. By definition, *contrast* is the difference between the darkest and lightest areas in a photo — the greater the difference, the higher the contrast. Photos with low contrast can appear a bit muddy or blurred, without any clear distinctions between details in the images.

Contrast in black-and-white photos works a bit differently than contrast in color photos. Grayscale images display contrast in terms of brightness levels,

or luminosity. Color images also have luminosity, but it shows up in color hue and saturation.

It is often amazing how a few tweaks of an image's hue and saturation levels can enhance contrast. Photoshop Elements includes several useful tools for adjusting image contrast, one of the best being the Levels dialog box. To open the Levels dialog box, click Enhance ⇨ Adjust Lighting ⇨ Levels. By making a few adjustments to the shadows, midtones, and highlights in a photo, you can quickly achieve contrast that was previously lacking.

In this photo, the lack of contrast results in a soft, almost blurred look to the trees.

In this example, the contrast is enhanced slightly by intensifying the highlights by sliding this slider to the left.

● Next, the shadows are intensified to create clearer contrast between the light and dark areas by sliding this slider to the right.

● The midtone slider can also be used to adjust contrast by clicking here and dragging toward the left or right.

Note the levels of intensities throughout the tonal range.

TIPS

Did You Know?

Learning to read the *histogram,* the graphical diagram in the Levels dialog box, is a great way to understand contrast issues in your photos. The histogram displays the tonal range of values in your image and shows you exactly where shadows, midtones, and highlights are at the strongest or weakest in the image. See Task #72 for more information.

Did You Know?

Sharpening filters can also help to improve the appearance of contrast in your photos. The most popular filter for sharpening images in Photoshop Elements is Unsharp Mask. Using this filter takes a bit of experimentation using the three available controls. To apply the filter, click Filter ⇨ Sharpen ⇨ Unsharp Mask. This opens the Unsharp Mask dialog box, in which you can make and preview adjustments.

IMPROVE IMAGE CONTRAST
by setting black and white points

You can use the Levels dialog box to specify black and white points within a photo. Targeting the darkest and brightest pixels in an image can help you restore image detail, tonal range, and contrast. After specifying new black and white points in an image, the full tonal range stretches out between the two settings to increase contrast. The result is often a dramatically improved image.

For example, when you target a white area in a photo, Photoshop Elements remaps and redefines the tonal information throughout the image, changing a

dingy image into one with clearer white and black areas. All the other pixel values in the image also adjust in proportion to the new highlight values.

The eyedropper tools help you target colors for highlights, shadows, and neutral grays. Because the tools target color changes, they work best for color correction problems rather than exposure problems. The key to setting black and white points is first identifying representative shadows and highlights in your image.

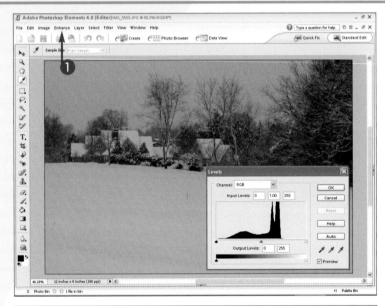

This photo lacks contrast and tonal range, with no clear white and dark pixels in the image.

1 Click Enhance.

2 Click Adjust Lighting.

3 Click Levels.

The Levels dialog box opens.

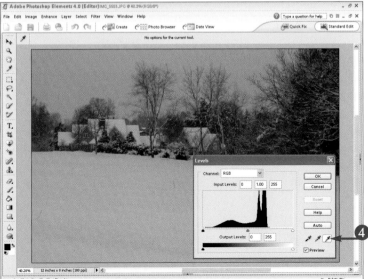

4 Click the Set White Point eyedropper.

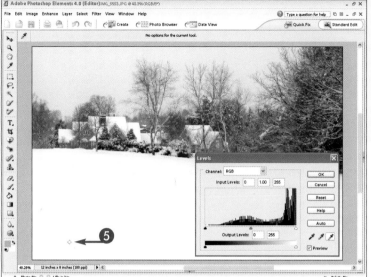

⑤ Click the whitest area in the image.

Photoshop Elements immediately establishes a new white point and adjusts other lighter pixels accordingly.

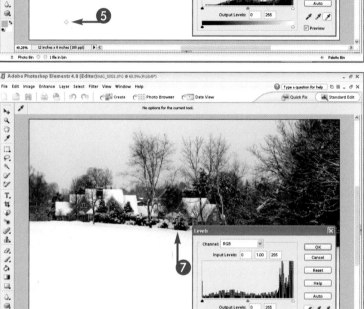

⑥ Click the Set Black Point eyedropper.

⑦ Click the blackest or darkest area in the image.

Elements immediately sets the new black point and adjusts the other darker pixels accordingly.

The photo now displays tonal range and improved contrast.

TIPS

Caution!

Be careful where you click the Levels eyedropper tools. If you click the Set White Point eyedropper over an area that is not representative of white in your photo, for example, other lighter tones in the image are affected and may become overly whitened. This may result in a loss of detail in your image and an excessively contrasty image. The same problem can occur if you click an area that is not truly black with the Set Black Point eyedropper. Picking the wrong areas when setting the black and white points can result in strange and inaccurate colors.

Did You Know?

You can use the Set Gray Point eyedropper in the Levels dialog box to assign neutral gray colors in an image. This eyedropper is not available for grayscale images.

IMPROVE IMAGE CONTRAST
with a Levels layer

You can create a Levels adjustment layer to improve the contrast in an image. You can use adjustment layers in Photoshop Elements to make changes to a photo without altering the underlying original image. With adjustment layers, you can apply all kinds of changes to color, tonal range, and contrast to a copy of the original image layer. The original image remains intact. After you are happy with your adjustments, you can flatten the image and apply the changes to the actual image layer. If you do not like the changes, you can simply discard the Levels adjustment layer. To learn more about creating adjustment layers, see Task #66.

A Levels adjustment layer is directly connected to the Levels dialog box. As such, you can easily summon the Levels dialog box at any time to make changes to the shadows, midtones, and highlights of an image. The Input sliders in the dialog box enable you to remap black and white points in your image to make improvements to the image's overall contrast.

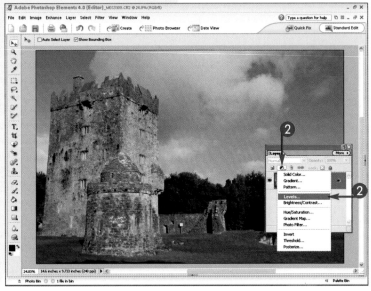

This photo appears a bit dull and lacking in contrast.

① Display the Layers palette.

Note: You can activate the Layers palette from the palette well or click Window ➪ Layers.

② Click here and select Levels.

Elements adds a new adjustment layer to the Layers palette, and the Levels dialog box opens.

③ Drag the Input Levels highlight slider to just inside of where the lightest image information begins.

The pixels in the highlights immediately lighten.

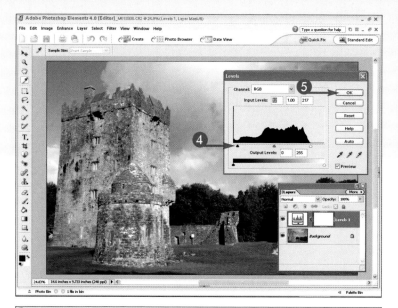

4 Drag the Input Levels shadow slider to the right a small amount.

The pixels in the shadow areas immediately darken.

5 Click OK.

DIFFICULTY LEVEL

Elements applies the changes made in the adjustment layer, and the photo's contrast improves.

● To return to the Levels dialog box at any time for more adjustments, simply double-click the Levels thumbnail.

● To switch between the before and after image, click the eye icon to turn on or off the visibility of the adjustment layer.

TIPS

Did You Know?
To keep your edits organized, consider naming any new adjustment layers that you add to the Layers palette. For example, if you use a Levels adjustment layer to correct contrast problems, name the layer "Contrast" to remind you of the purpose of the layer. To name a layer, double-click the default layer name in the Layers palette and type a new name. Press Enter, and Elements saves the new name.

Did You Know?
You can apply an adjustment layer to part of your image instead of the entire image. To do so, make a selection with a selection tool before creating the adjustment layer.

REVEAL HIGHLIGHT DETAIL #78
with the Shadows/Highlights command

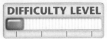
DIFFICULTY LEVEL

If your photo suffers from an overexposed background, such as a sky that is brighter than the subject matter, you can make corrections using the Shadows/Highlights command. This command enables you to reduce the brightness from the sun or other reflective light sources and to bring out background details. For example, reducing the brightness of the sky in some photos can reveal details in clouds.

The Shadows/Highlights filter works by darkening overexposed areas in an image. Tonal variations for this filter are measured in values that range from 0 to 100. The larger the value setting number, the darker the image's background appears.

If you prefer to keep the foreground or subject matter unaffected by the filter, select it and copy it to another layer in the Layers palette before applying this technique to the layer containing the overexposed background.

To precisely fix exposure problems, you can use the Levels dialog box to fine-tune the shadows, midtones, and highlights.

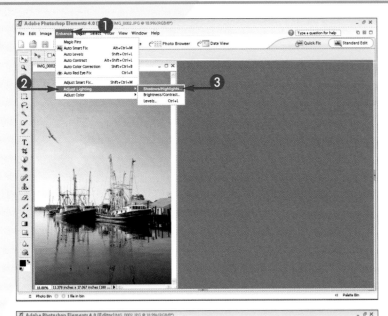

❶ Click Enhance.

❷ Click Adjust Lighting.

❸ Click Shadows/Highlights.

The Shadows/Highlights dialog box opens.

❹ Click and drag the Darken Highlights slider to bring out the cloud detail in the sky.

❺ Click OK.

Photoshop Elements applies your adjustments.

REVEAL SHADOW DETAIL
with the Shadows/Highlights command

#79

You can use the Shadows/Highlights filter in Photoshop Elements to lighten the shadows in a photo. Pictures that you take in bright light often produce very dark shadows in the foreground objects, resulting in very little detail. For example, if you take a picture of someone against a bright background, the person's face often turns into a silhouette with shadows obscuring the details of his face. Using the Shadows/Highlights filter, you can

bring out the shadow details and enhance the overall image appearance.

With the Shadows/Highlights command, you can create the illusion of a *fill flash,* which professional photographers use to fill in light for darker lighting conditions. You can use this command to adjust photos that suffer from poor foreground lighting.

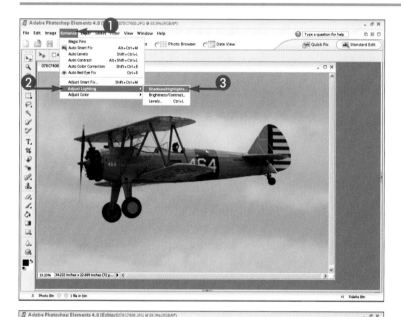

In this photo, a lot of details on the plane are lost in the shadows.

① Click Enhance.

② Click Adjust Lighting.

③ Click Shadows/Highlights.

The Shadows/Highlights dialog box opens.

④ Click and drag the Lighten Shadows slider to increase the shadow lighting.

⑤ Click OK.

The plane's details now appear more clearly.

LIGHTEN OR DARKEN
a selected portion of an image

In some cases, only certain areas of your photo may need lightening or darkening to improve the photo's appearance. Perhaps only a portion of someone's face needs lightening or a specific highlight needs toning down. You can select an area of your photo to edit in Photoshop Elements and then make adjustments to the shadows, midtones, and highlights using the Levels dialog box. The remaining portions of the image are not affected by any changes that you apply.

Depending on the level of detail in your photo, you may find selecting a specific portion of the image for edits time-consuming. Photoshop Elements offers a variety of selection tools to assist you. To learn more about using the selection tools in the toolbox, see Task #64.

For the best results, make a copy of the background or other layer that you want to edit, and then make your changes to the layer copy. This leaves the original photo layer intact in case you do not like the results of your changes.

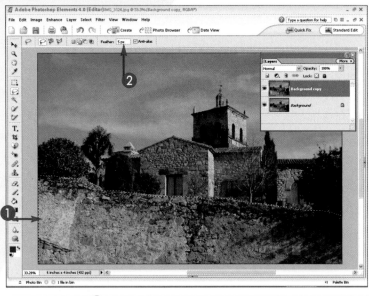

① Use a selection tool to select the area or portion of the photo that you want to edit.

② Set Feather to 5px to make a soft edge selection.

③ Click Enhance.

④ Click Adjust Lighting.

⑤ Click Levels.

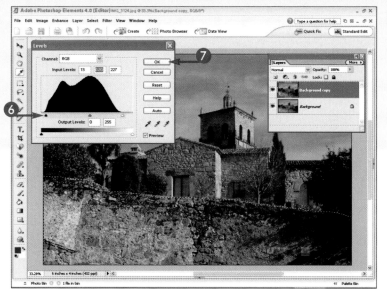

The Levels dialog box opens.

6 Click and drag the shadows, midtones, or highlights sliders to lighten or darken the selected portion of the photo.

This example shows increased contrast in the foreground wall while the building and sky remain the same.

7 Click OK.

DIFFICULTY LEVEL

Photoshop Elements applies your changes to the photo.

8 Click Select.

9 Click Deselect.

The selection marquee is removed.

Did You Know?

You can quickly create an inverse of a selected area in a photo to select the remaining portion of the image. To do so, click Select ➪ Inverse.

Did You Know?

You can save yourself some time and effort by saving your selections. For example, if you painstakingly trace a detailed subject in a photo, you can save the selection to reuse again with other edits. To save a selection, click Select ➪ Save Selection. The Save Selection dialog box opens. In this dialog box, type a name for the selection and click OK. To reuse the selection again, click Select ➪ Load Selection and specify which selection to apply.

REMOVE A COLOR CAST
with the Color Cast command

One of the most common color problems from which photos can suffer is unwanted color cast. This problem frequently occurs when shooting indoor scenes with improper ambient lighting using the wrong color balance setting on a digital camera. The result is often a photo with a displeasing tint. You can also introduce color cast problems by shooting in colored light, such as that found early in the morning or near sunset. In many cases, these color casts are favorable, and in other cases, they need to be removed. Photoshop Elements includes several tools for eliminating color cast problems. This task focuses

on using the Remove Color Cast command to correct unwanted color casts.

The key to using the Remove Color Cast command is to apply it to areas of the image that should be gray, white, or black. Doing so causes Photoshop Elements to change the overall mixture of colors in the image to compensate for the improper color cast. Photoshop Elements checks the sampled area to which you applied it and adds equal amounts of red, green, and blue. Elements also shifts the remaining colors to create a neutral state.

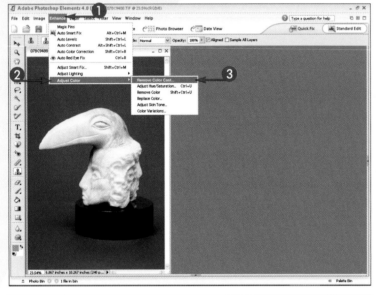

REMOVE A BLUE COLOR CAST

In this example, the photo has a bluish color cast.

1 Click Enhance.

2 Click Adjust Color.

3 Click Remove Color Cast.

The Remove Color Cast dialog box appears.

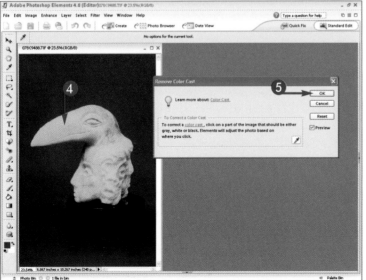

4 Click an area in the image that should be gray, white, or black.

Note: Clicking a white area in the image produces a warmer color cast.

5 Click OK.

Photoshop Elements removes the blue color cast.

REMOVE A GREEN COLOR CAST

In this photo, the green colors in the leaves and ferns give the image a greenish cast.

① Perform the earlier steps **1** to **4**.

DIFFICULTY LEVEL

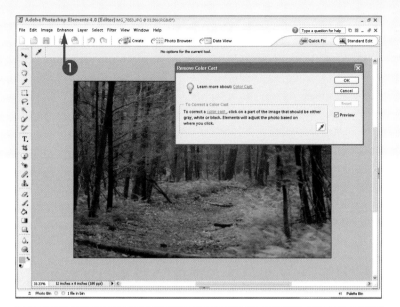

② Click OK.

Photoshop Elements applies the changes to the photo.

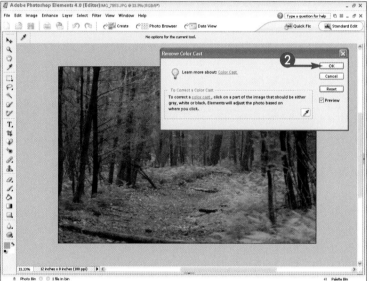

TIP

Did You Know?

Sometimes, you can use the Color Variations feature to correct simple color cast problems — and to add a pleasant color cast such as the warm glow that you often see near sunset. The Color Variations feature enables you to adjust color balance, contrast, and saturation. To use this feature, click Enhance ⇨ Adjust Color ⇨ Color Variations. This opens the Color Variations dialog box. Next, click a tonal range to apply adjustments to different tones in your image. To add a color or subtract a color, click one of the thumbnails. The After preview area shows the results. You can continue clicking the thumbnail to increase or decrease the adjustment.

ADJUST COLOR
with a Hue/Saturation layer

You can create a Hue/Saturation adjustment layer to make adjustments to the colors in a photo. You use the Hue/Saturation filter controls to change the hue of a photo, to increase or decrease color saturation throughout the image, or to adjust the lightness values of the colors. A Hue/Saturation adjustment layer is directly connected to the Hue/Saturation dialog box.

The Hue level control enables you to change colors based on Elements's color wheel and set different color hues. Moving the control's slider represents a move around the color wheel. The Saturation control enables you to adjust the purity or intensity of the colors. The Lightness control lets you set a brightness level for the colors.

You can choose to edit all the colors at once, or you can edit preset color ranges, such as the yellow or green colors in a photo. The Master setting encompasses all the colors in a photo and appears by default in the Hue/Saturation dialog box. To edit a specific color instead, you must first specify the color before adjusting the slider controls.

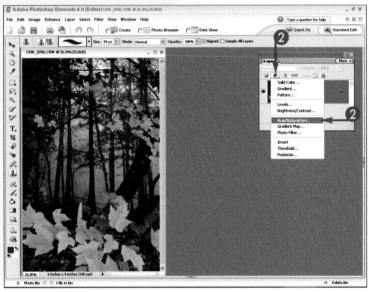

① Display the Layers palette.

Note: You can activate the Layers palette from the palette well, or click Window ➪ Layers.

② Click the Create Adjustment Layer button in the Layers palette and choose Hue/Saturation.

Note: See Task #66 to learn more about adjustment layers.

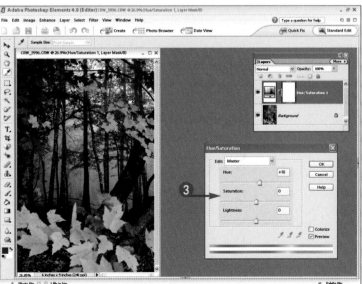

Elements adds a new adjustment layer to the Layers palette, and the Hue/Saturation dialog box opens.

③ Click and drag a slider to adjust the hue, saturation, or lightness.

In this example, the Hue slider changes the color of the image, particularly the leaves.

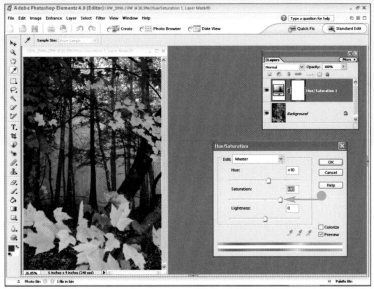

● In this example, the saturation level is increased to intensify the colors.

● To edit specific colors in the image, click here and select a color.

④ Click OK.

Photoshop Elements applies the changes to the layer.

TIPS

Did You Know?

You can use the Levels dialog box to intensify selected color channels in an image. For example, if you want to boost the colors in the Red channel only, you can specify the channel first and then adjust the shadows, midtones, and highlights sliders. See Task #77 to learn how to create a Levels adjustment layer.

Did You Know?

You can also use the Multiply blending mode to strengthen colors in a photo. Duplicate the layer that you want to adjust and then apply the Multiply blending mode by clicking the blending mode button in the Layers palette and selecting Multiply. You can then adjust the color intensity of the effect with the Opacity control.

Make Photographic Prints

Even though taking pictures with a digital camera makes it easy to share digital photos electronically — on a Web page, as an e-mail attachment, or on a computer or TV screen — a photographic print on paper is still what photography is all about to many people. You can make photo-quality prints from digital photo files in many ways, including printing them on a desktop photo printer, ordering prints from an online photo-printing service, or using a local photo-processing lab.

Before you are ready to make prints, however, you may need to perform some basic image editing to get the best results. To make prints that look like the images on your computer

screen, you need to take the time to calibrate your monitor with Adobe Gamma or a monitor-calibration device.

Besides making basic photo corrections to your digital photos, you also need to make sure that the aspect ratio is correct for the print size you want, that the image size is large enough for the print size, and that the photo has been sharpened for the target printer. If you are using your own desktop photo printer, you may also want to use Adobe Photoshop Elements or another image editor to precisely position photos on a page, create multiple photo page layouts, or crop photos that will be printed in a book using an online printing service.

Top 100

Understanding
COLOR MANAGEMENT

Your digital camera, computer screen, and printer all reproduce color differently, and each one has different limitations on how it can display color. Color management is a system of hardware and software products that have been configured to ensure accurate color across all devices. In other words, if you have implemented color management properly on your hardware, the barn-red barn in front of the soft, pale blue sky that you see on your computer monitor will actually show up as barn red against the same soft, pale blue sky in your prints.

A couple important steps in color managing your hardware are calibrating your computer display and using the right color profiles for the specific combination of printer, ink, and paper that you are using. Taking, editing, and printing digital photos can be a joy and easy to do when you have accurate color across your hardware and software. Without color management, the same process of taking, editing, and printing digital photos can become frustrating, causing you to waste money on paper and ink by creating unacceptable prints.

The LCD screen on the Canon PowerShot G3 displays a thumbnail image of a photo of a few orchids.

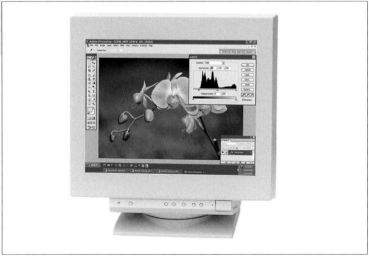

This computer monitor displays the orchids as they looked when the photo was taken.

This print of the orchids looks the same as it did on the monitor and as it looked when the photo was taken.

83

DIFFICULTY LEVEL

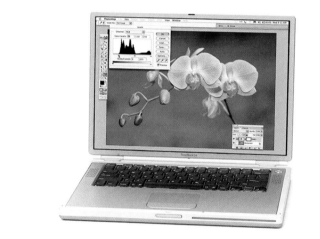

The orchids on this Mac PowerBook G4 LCD look the same as they did on the print, on the PC monitor, and when the photo was taken.

TIPS

Did You Know?

You can calibrate your Windows PC monitor using Adobe Gamma, which is a software utility added to the Control Panel when you install Adobe Photoshop Elements. To access the Control Panel, click the Start button and select Control Panel from the menu. If you are using a Mac, you can use Apple's ColorSync utility, which can be found in System Preferences. Be sure to adjust your monitor in the lighting conditions that you normally work in.

Did You Know?

The most accurate way to calibrate your computer monitor or LCD is to use a monitor spider such as the MonacoOPTIX^{XR} Colorimeter for LCD and CRT displays (www.xritephoto.com). This hardware product attaches to your computer display so that it can read colors displayed by the monitor and create an accurate color profile.

CROP A PHOTO
to a specified size

You can crop your photos when you want to keep only a certain part of them or when you need to make a photo meet specific width and height requirements. Adobe Photoshop Elements offers two useful tools for cropping images — the Rectangular Marquee and Crop tools. First, you can select the part of the image that you want to keep using the Rectangular Marquee tool and then select Image ➪ Crop to crop the image. Alternatively, you can use the Crop tool, which has a few extra features that

are useful for cropping images precisely as you want them.

Using the Crop tool, not only can you crop to a fixed aspect ratio, but you can also crop to a fixed size, specified in inches, and at a specified printer resolution. Additionally, the Crop tool enables you to drag the edges of a selection to select exactly the area that you want; it even enables you to rotate the image if needed.

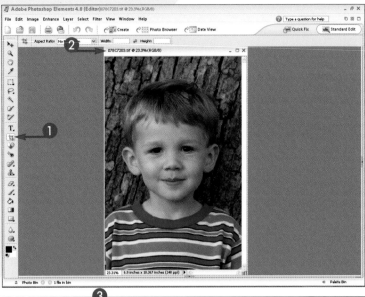

① Click the Crop tool.

② Double-click the document title bar to maximize the document window to make cropping easy.

③ Click here and select the aspect ratio.

● Alternatively, you can type in the width and height that you want.

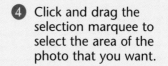

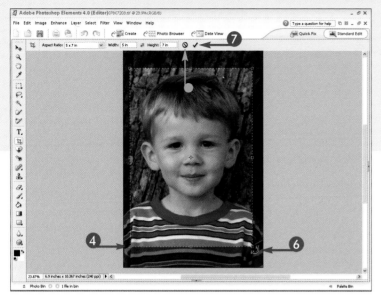

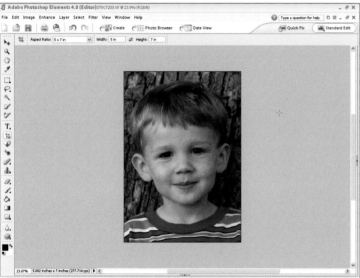

4 Click and drag the selection marquee to select the area of the photo that you want.

5 Place the mouse pointer outside a corner of the selection marquee.

The cursor changes to indicate that you can rotate the image.

6 Click and drag to rotate the selection until it appears as you like it.

7 Click here to apply the crop.

● To cancel the crop, click here.

The image is cropped, resized, and rotated as chosen.

84

DIFFICULTY LEVEL

TIPS

Did You Know?

You can increase or decrease the size of the selection by clicking one of the corners of the selection marquee and dragging it. If you entered values in the Width and Height box, the Crop tool automatically maintains the aspect ratio.

You can move the entire selection marquee by clicking inside the marquee and dragging the cursor.

If you want to crop to the outside of the photo, click outside the photo and drag the selection marquee to where you want it to be.

Caution!

When you crop an image, its resolution is lowered. You can use Image Size ➪ Resize Image Size to set the resolution.

Make a
LARGE PRINT

The largest size print you can make with your digital camera is limited by the pixel size of your camera, the quality of the photo you want to enlarge, and your tolerance for image degradation due to image upsampling. A 4-megapixel camera has more pixels than a 3-megapixel camera and can therefore generally be used to make larger prints. Images with low digital noise and smooth tonal gradations are better candidates to use for large prints than images taken at high ISO settings with lots of digital noise — unless the intent is to get that effect.

To determine how large a print you can make with any given image, you need to experiment and examine the prints. To determine the optimal print size, you divide the pixel dimensions by the optimal print PPI for the printer or print service you intend to use. For example, most Epson printers make excellent prints at 240PPI. Hence, a 3.3-megapixel image that provides a 1,536 x 2,480 pixel image would make an *optimal* print size of 6.4" x 10.3" — enough for an excellent 5"x 7" print, but not quite enough for an 8" x 10" print.

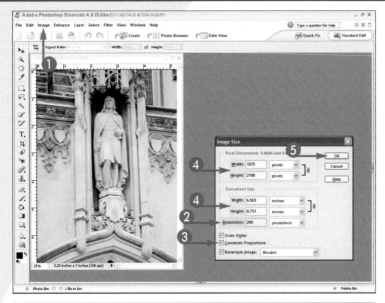

① Click Image ⇨ Resize ⇨ Image Size.

The Image Size dialog box appears.

② Type the target printer PPI in the Resolution box.

③ Make sure that a check mark is in the Constrain Proportions box to keep the aspect ratio constant.

④ Type the width or height that you want in either the Pixel Dimensions area or the Document size area.

⑤ Click OK.

The image size is changed.

The optimal print size is 1,575 x 2,100 pixels at 240PPI.

This 9.46MB image is the optimal print size, and it shows no loss in image quality.

This photo has been upsampled to be 1,920 x 2,560 pixels, which makes an 8" x 10" print at 240PPI.

A noticeable but acceptable amount of image degradation is visible in this 26.5MB image.

This photo has been upsampled to be 3840 x 5120 pixels, which makes a 16" x 20" print at 240PPI.

Substantial and unacceptable image degradation, caused by overincreasing the image size, appears in this 56.3MB image.

TIPS

Did You Know?

When resizing images using the Image Size feature, you need to be careful to choose the most appropriate resampling algorithm. Use Bicubic Smoother when enlarging an image and Bicubic Sharper when reducing the size of an image.

Caution!

When enlarging any image, you should always save the upsampled image to a new file and not overwrite the original image. Writing over the original image leaves you with nothing but the lesser-quality image.

SHARPEN
a digital image

Most photos taken with digital cameras look soft; that is, they do not look as sharply focused as they could. This is primarily due to the fact that digital cameras capture "digitally" instead of in an analog fashion like film cameras, with which it is easier to capture the important details found on the edges of elements in a photo.

However, using an image editor such as Photoshop Elements, you can make an image look as sharp as any photo taken with a film camera. One easy way to

increase the perceived sharpness of a photo is to use the Unsharp Mask filter found in most image-editing applications.

You need to use different Unsharp Mask settings for the same photo when using it in different sizes for different purposes. For example, the best settings for an 800 x 640–pixel image that you want to use on a Web page are entirely different than the settings you need to make a high-resolution print on an inkjet printer.

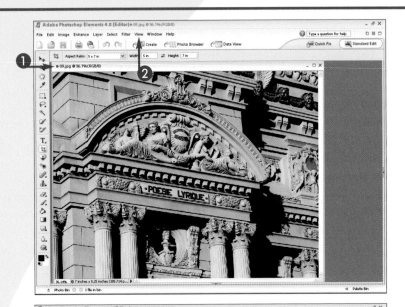

❶ Double-click the document title bar to maximize the image.

❷ Click View.

❸ Click Actual Pixels.

The image is shown at full size.

❹ Click the Hand tool.

❺ Click and drag the image to view a portion where sharpening is critical.

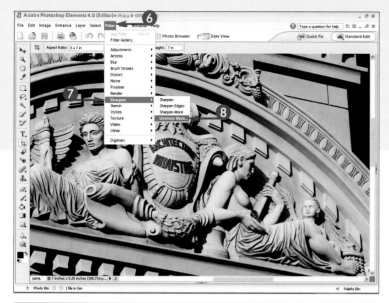

#86

DIFFICULTY LEVEL

6 Click Filter.

7 Click Sharpen.

8 Click Unsharp Mask.

The Unsharp Mask dialog box appears.

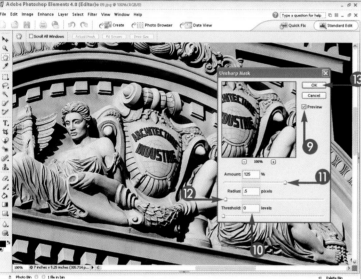

9 Make sure that the Preview box is checked.

10 First set Amount to 175, Radius to 1, and Threshold to 0.

11 Drag the Amount slider left or right until the image looks sharp.

12 Drag the Radius slider left or right to further improve the image sharpness.

13 Click OK.

The image is sharpened as you have specified.

Did You Know?

You cannot use Photoshop Elements to sharpen a poorly focused digital photo. The Unsharp Mask filter only increases the perceived sharpness of an already well-focused photo. If you want a good photo that appears "tack sharp," you must first shoot it in focus and then apply the Unsharp Mask filter to get the best results.

Did You Know?

You cannot determine the best settings to use to make a photographic print when using Unsharp Mask by examining the results on your computer screen. Although it is best to examine the effects at full image resolution when using a computer screen, you can best determine the success or failure of your settings by making a print and examining it carefully.

PRECISELY POSITION PHOTOS
on a page

You may have many reasons to precisely position one or more photos on a page. Maybe you want to create your own print portfolio, a scrapbook page, or a greeting card. Whatever the reason, you can take several approaches. Depending on the printer that you use, your printer software may have a feature that enables you to specify exactly where an image should be printed on the page. If you are printing a page with only one photo, using your printer software may be the best approach.

You can use the Photoshop Elements Image ⇨ Resize ⇨ Canvas Size command to "add paper" around an open image when you want only a single photo on a page. To use this feature, you need to calculate the amount of paper to add to each side. Or you can create a new blank page and drag and drop one or more open photos onto the new page and place them where you want using the Ruler feature, as shown in this task.

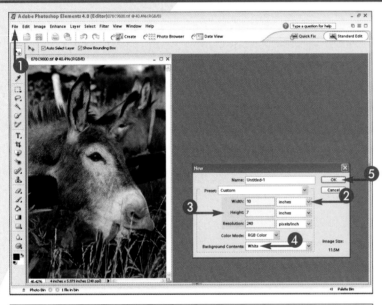

① Click File ⇨ New ⇨ Blank File.

The New dialog box appears.

② Click here and select Inches.

③ Type the width, height, and resolution for the target printer.

④ Make sure that Background Contents is set to White.

⑤ Click OK.

Elements creates a new document to your specifications.

⑥ Click the Move tool.

⑦ Click and drag the photo that you want to place to the new, blank document.

The photo appears in the new document.

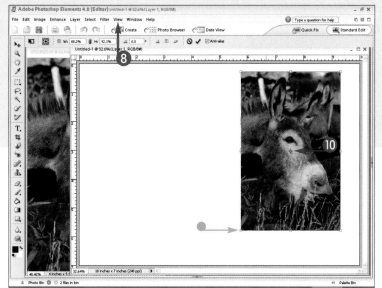

DIFFICULTY LEVEL

⑧ Click View.

⑨ Click Rulers.

The rulers appear in the new document window.

⑩ Click the photo layer with the Move tool to move the image where you want it.

● If you click and drag the handles around the photo, you can change the size of the image. Press Shift while dragging to maintain the aspect ratio.

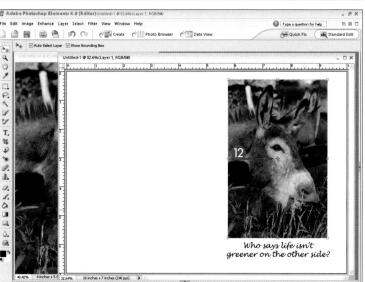

⑪ Press Ctrl + + (plus sign) to increase the zoom (or Ctrl + − [minus sign] to decrease the zoom) so that you have a larger and more precise ruler.

⑫ Drag the photo with the Move tool until you have the image positioned as you want it.

You can move the image up, down, and sideways by pressing the arrow keys. Each press moves the image one pixel.

TIPS

Did You Know?

When you drag and drop, or when you cut and paste, multiple images onto a blank page, the images are all placed on their own layers. To view and select these layers, open the Layers palette. You can easily add any one of many varieties of drop shadows or other effects by opening the Layer Styles palette and double-clicking the style of your choice.

Did You Know?

Each time that you place a new image on a page as a layer, you increase the size of the file. To flatten the layers, click Layer ➪ Flatten Image. First, save the file as a PSD file if you want to save the layers for future editing. When you place text on an image, a text layer is created, and text layers can be flattened as well.

PRINT MULTIPLE PHOTOS
on a page

You can save photo paper, printer ink, and money by creating a multiphoto layout and printing more than one photo per page. Although you can do this manually by using several of the features found in Adobe Photoshop Elements, the Print Multiple Photos command lets you quickly and easily make multiphoto prints that are similar to school photo pages.

Besides using one of the 20 preformatted pages, you can also customize your own layout. You can learn more about making customized layouts by consulting the Adobe Photoshop Elements Help system. You can also automatically make a multiphoto print of every photo in a selected folder. The Picture Package's default layout is for multiple copies of a single photo. After you have selected a layout, however, you can click each photo and pick another photo to fill that space.

① Open the digital photo that you want to use to make a multiphoto print and click it to make it the active document.

② Click File.

③ Click Print Multiple Photos.

The Adobe Organizer is launched, and the Print Photos dialog box appears.

④ Click here and select Picture Package.

⑤ Click here and select a layout.

⑥ Click here and select your printer.

⑦ Click here to check the box to print the same photo on the page.

8 Click Add to add the images.

9 Uncheck the Fill Page With First Photo check box to print different photos on a page.

10 If you want to use a media profile, click More Options.

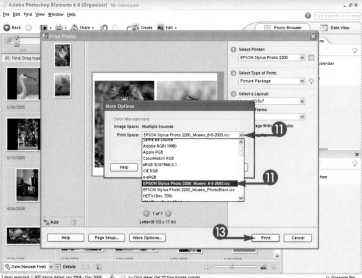

The More Options dialog box appears.

11 Click here and select your media profile.

12 Click OK.

13 Click Print.

The printing process begins.

TIPS

Time-Saver!

When you use the Photoshop Elements Print Photos dialog box, you will need to cut each photo from the page. If your photo-quality printer has a borderless print feature, make sure to check Borderless in the Print Photos dialog box. This will save you time in cutting the photos.

Did You Know?

You can use the Photoshop Elements Print Photos dialog box to make photo labels, photo tags, and more. Just click in the Select Type of Print box and choose Labels. The formats provided match Avery's labels. To learn more about these labels, visit www.avery.com.

Order
PRINTS ONLINE

If you enjoy using a one-hour photo-finishing service at a local photo lab, you may enjoy using one of the online printing services such as the Kodak EasyShare Gallery, which is now built into Photoshop Elements. Although it is not possible to get your photo prints back in an hour, you can select, edit, upload, and order photo prints from your computer any time you like — without the hassles of going to a local lab to drop off your photos and to pick them up. After uploading your photos to an online printing service, your photos are printed and delivered to your mailbox within a few days.

Besides being able to order prints for yourself after you have uploaded them, you can also send a link via e-mail to anyone else with whom you want to share the photos. They can view the photos online in a Web browser; if they want, they can order prints themselves at their own expense, or you can order prints to mail to them. Besides just ordering photo prints at competitive prices, you can also have your photos printed in photo albums or books — or on hats, greeting cards, calendars, and many other photo objects.

① Using Adobe Organizer, open the folder containing the images that you want to print.

② Click Edit ➪ Select All to select all the images.

A blue border appears around all the images.

③ Click File ➪ Order Prints.

If you have not yet signed up for the Kodak EasyShare service, follow the instructions to do so.

The Adobe Photoshop Services dialog box appears.

④ Click one of these check boxes to select single or double prints of all the photos.

⑤ Click and drag the scroll bar to see more photos and change the size and quantity to order for each photo.

⑥ Click Next.

The Recipients page appears.

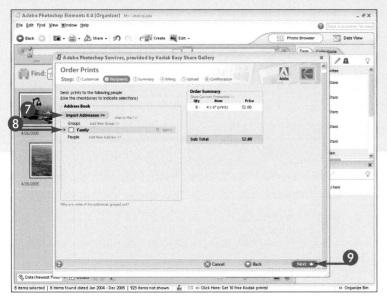

⑦ Click Import Addresses to add a new address.

⑧ Click an address's check box to choose that as the photo recipient.

⑨ Click Next to get the Summary page.

⑩ Review the summary to make sure that the information is accurate.

⑪ Click Next to get the Billing page.

⑫ Verify the billing information.

⑬ Click Place Order to begin the upload process.

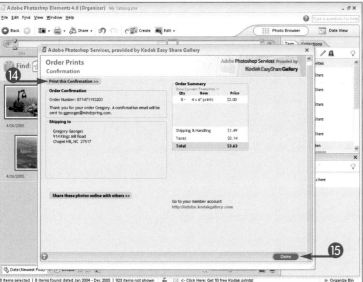

After the photos have been uploaded, the Confirmation page appears.

⑭ Click Print This Confirmation to print a copy of the confirmation information on your printer.

⑮ Click Done.

Within a few minutes, you will receive an e-mail confirming the order details.

TIPS

Did You Know?

The best way to use an online photo-printing service is to crop, edit, and place all the photos that you want into a single folder before uploading them to the service. Crop each of the photos to the aspect ratio of the print size that you will want to order and save them in an appropriate file format.

Did You Know?

Other online photo-printing services you may want to consider in addition to Kodak EasyShare (www.kodakgallery.com) are ezprints (www.ezprints.com), ImageStation (www.imagestation.com), and Shutterfly (www.shutterfly.com).

If you are using a Macintosh, you can upload and order photo prints and photo books easily by using Apple's iPhoto photo application or any of the other online photo-processing services that enable you to upload via a Web browser.

Create and order a
PHOTO BOOK ONLINE

Making a printed photo book is one of the most exciting ways to share photographs. The next time that you have a family get-together, you can create printed photo books and make them available to your family members. Or you may want to make your own 12" x 16" hardcover coffee table book featuring your top 40 photos.

One of the leading online photo book companies is MyPublisher. A significant part of the MyPublisher service is the free software that you use to create your books. To download the MyPublisher BookMaker software, visit www.mypublisher.com.

MyPublisher offers 6" x 8" pocket books with 20 pages and up to 80 photos for only $9.95. You can add additional pages for only $0.49 each. MyPublisher's 9" x 12" hardcover photo books with 20 pages and up to 160 photos are only $29.80, and you can add additional pages for only $1.49 each. And if you want a really big book, MyPublisher offers giant 12" x 16" full-bleed books with edge-to-edge printing, plus a hardcover binding made of imported linen for only $3 per page. A 20-page book costs around $60.

❶ Using BookMaker, click Get Photos.

❷ Click From Folder.

❸ Click the folder that contains the images you want to print in a book.

Thumbnail images are created and displayed.

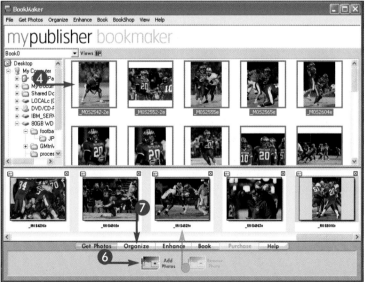

❹ To add all the photos to the book, first click the first photo.

❺ Press and hold Shift while clicking the last photo.

All the thumbnail images now show a blue border.

❻ Click Add Photos to add all the selected photos to the book.

⬤ Thumbnail images appear here.

❼ Click Organize.

The Organize page appears.

8 To choose a theme, click here and select a theme style.

9 To choose a template, click here and select a template style.

10 Click Single-Sided Printing or Double-Sided Printing.

The pages are automatically created using the selected settings.

11 Click Enhance.

The Enhance page appears.

12 Click an image's thumbnail to choose it to enhance.

13 Click one or more of the buttons to choose an enhancement feature.

14 Click Undo if you want to undo an enhancement to an image.

The edited image is displayed.

15 Click Book.

90

DIFFICULTY LEVEL

TIP

Did You Know?

If you want to make your own photo books using the paper of your choice and a desktop inkjet printer, you can do so by purchasing a photo book cover made for this purpose. In particular, ArtZ's (www.artzproducts.com) coffee table books and Red River Paper's (www.redriverpaper.com) custom book kits make excellent photo books that can feature your photos printed on your favorite inkjet paper, using a color profile — and printed to perfection. The innovative "self-binding" features of these and other photo books will provide you with a photo book that you will be pleased with.

Create and order a
PHOTO BOOK ONLINE

If you do not want to order a photo book online, you can purchase StoryTeller from Epson (www.epson.com) and make your own photo book using your inkjet printer. Epson's StoryTeller is a kit that comes with album software, paper, a book, and a glossy cover. StoryTeller enables you to choose from 18 book covers and 60 page layouts.

After you have printed all the photos on the pages, you can add your favorite photos to the glossy book

cover to make a fine-looking book. Extra sheets and one extra cover are included to ensure that you successfully complete your book.

The 5" x 7" StoryTeller photo book creator with 10 pages is $19.99, the 8" x 10" photo book with 10 pages is $24.99, and you can get a 20-page 8" x 10" photo album, too, for $29.99.

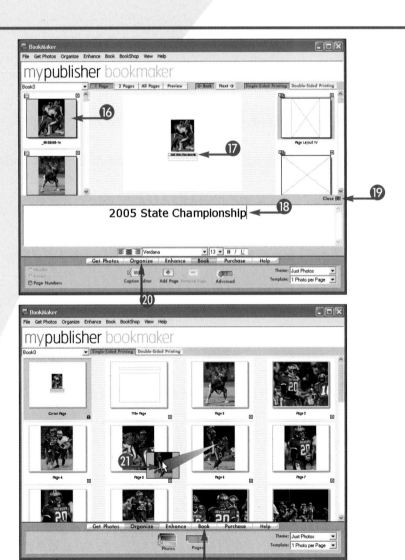

The Book page appears.

⑯ Click the first image to select the title page.

⑰ Click here to select the first line of text.

⑱ Click here and type the title text.

⑲ Click Close.

The text box closes, and the text is applied to the page.

⑳ Click Organize again.

The Organize page appears again.

㉑ Click and drag the images that you want to move to new locations.

㉒ Click Book again.

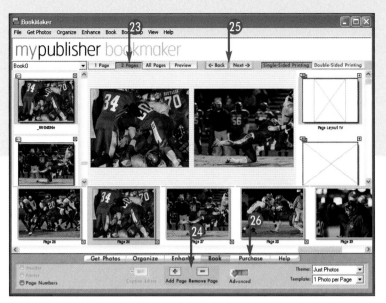

The Book page appears again.

㉓ Click 2 Pages to get a two-page view.

㉔ Click Add Page or Remove Page to add or remove pages.

㉕ Click Next or Back to preview each of the pages.

㉖ Click Purchase.

90
CONTINUED

The first Purchase page appears.

㉗ Complete the ordering process to begin uploading the photos to the MyPublisher online printing service.

Within a few days, your printed book will be delivered to you.

Apply It!
Choose a cover image and cover text to make a perfect book like this one when using MyPublisher's online printing service.

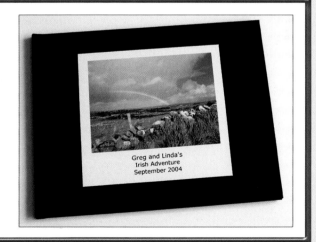

Complete Digital Photo Projects

After you have taken a few good photos and edited them, you are ready to use your photos in digital photo projects. Two good digital photo projects to start with are organizing your digital photo collection with an image manager and archiving your valuable digital photo collection to external drives or offline storage media. After you have organized and archived your digital photo collection, you are ready to complete more digital photo projects.

One of the most exciting aspects of digital photography is that you can easily share and enjoy your digital photos in so many ways. You can attach one or more photos to e-mail, create slideshows to show on your computer screen or even on a TV screen, publish online

photo galleries, create digital photo albums, make collages, and more.

Many digital photo projects require software beyond what you use to edit photos. With increased interest in digital photography, the marketplace offers an incredible number of products from which to choose. Often you can choose one software product that enables you to complete most or all of your projects. Some of the more feature-rich and easy-to-use products include Adobe Photoshop Elements (www.adobe.com), Apple iPhoto (www.apple.com), Corel Paint Shop Pro (www.corel.com), Roxio Easy CD & DVD Creator (www.roxio.com), Roxio PhotoSuite Platinum Edition (www.roxio.com), and Ulead PhotoImpact (www.ulead.com).

Top 100

ORGANIZE
your digital photos

After you have stored a few hundred of your digital photos on your computer, you will need an effective way to organize and manage your growing digital photo collection. Software products that enable you to easily manage large digital photo collections are called *image managers,* and there are a number of good ones available. One of the more powerful and easy-to-use image managers is Cerious Software's ThumbsPlus, which you can download from www.cerious.com.

After you pick one or more folders or a drive to manage, ThumbsPlus automatically creates thumbnail images for every digital photo file in the selected folders or drives. In addition to viewing the images quickly by looking at the thumbnails, you can also view a variety of textual information, such as the EXIF data that image files may contain. To learn more about working with EXIF data, see Task #46.

ThumbsPlus not only keeps a database of the filenames and thumbnail images, but also acts as a repository for a variety of other useful textual information. You can add keywords to photos, save location information, add annotations, copyright information, and much more.

VIEW IMAGES AND IMAGE INFORMATION

① Click a folder to view the images that it contains.

● The Preview and Info tabs display details about the selected image or images.

● Thumbnail images display user-selected information below.

② Click the Info tab to display user-selected information about the image selected in the thumbnail area.

The user-selected information shows camera settings such as f-stop, shutter speed, ISO, and focal length.

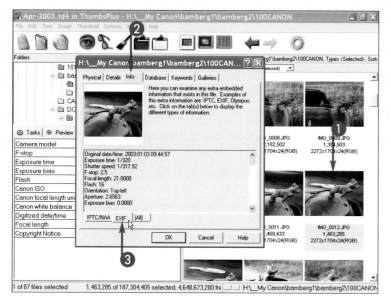

VIEW EXIF DATA

1. Right-click a thumbnail image and click Properties on the menu that appears.

   The Properties dialog box appears.

2. Click the Info tab.

3. Click EXIF.

   The EXIF data appears.

91

DIFFICULTY LEVEL

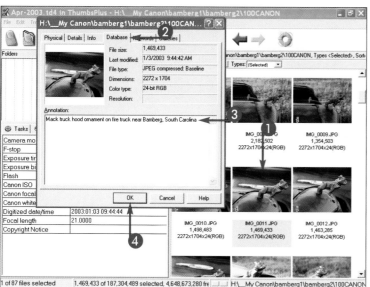

ANNOTATE AN IMAGE

1. Right-click a thumbnail image and click Properties on the menu that appears.

   The Properties dialog box appears.

2. Click the Database tab.

3. Type your comments.

4. Click OK.

   Your annotation is saved with the image's information.

TIPS

Did You Know?

ThumbsPlus offers many features for viewing digital photos. Besides being able to scale the thumbnails and view more or fewer of them at a time, you can also choose a list or report view, which you can customize to show just the textual information that you want. You can also open more than one copy of ThumbsPlus at a time. This enables you to drag and drop photos from one folder to another while viewing the contents of more than one folder.

Did You Know?

When you want to carefully compare two or more digital photos side by side, you can click File ➪ View Synched. The synch view enables you to scroll right or left in one image and simultaneously scroll in the other images.

ORGANIZE
your digital photos

Many software vendors who initially created image managers have realized the value of adding features that not only increase your ability to organize and manage your digital photo collection, but also take advantage of a considerable number of project features such as slideshows, Web galleries, contact sheets, printed image catalogs, and much more. A few of the more feature-rich and easy-to-use image managers with useful project features are the following:

ACDSee (www.acdsystems.com)

Adobe Photoshop Elements (www.adobe.com)

Apple iPhoto (www.apple.com)

Cerious Software ThumbsPlus (www.cerious.com)

Corel Paint Shop Pro (www.corel.com)

Ulead PhotoImpact (www.ulead.com)

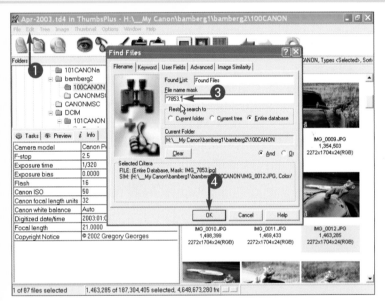

SEARCH FOR FILES BY NAME

① Click Edit.

② Click Find by Query.

   The Find Files dialog box appears.

③ Type a filename or a filename mask.

④ Click OK.

   ThumbsPlus searches for matching files and displays the thumbnails of the files that it finds.

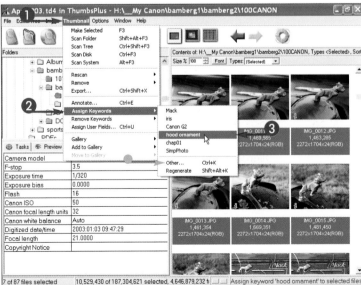

ASSIGN A KEYWORD FOR SEARCH QUERIES

① Click Thumbnail.

② Click Assign Keywords.

③ Click the keyword that you want to assign to the image to use for queries.

● Alternatively, you can click Other and add other keyword choices.

   The keywords are written to the ThumbsPlus database.

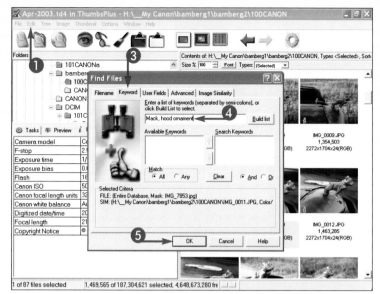

FIND AN IMAGE CONTAINING KEYWORDS

1 Click Edit.

2 Click Find by Query.

The Find Files dialog box appears.

3 Click the Keyword tab.

4 Type keywords, separated by commas.

5 Click OK.

A window displays all images with the selected keywords.

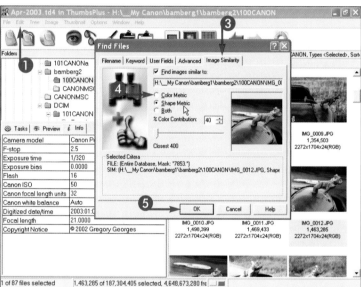

FIND A SIMILAR-LOOKING IMAGE

1 After clicking on an image to select it, click Edit.

2 Click Find by Query.

The Find Files dialog box appears.

3 Click the Image Similarity tab.

4 Specify similarity settings here.

5 Click OK.

ThumbsPlus displays a folder with images similar to the one that was initially selected.

Did You Know?

One of the most useful features found in ThumbsPlus is the Edit ➪ Find Similar Images command. You can use the Find Similar Image dialog box to find images that look similar based on a number of metrics, including color and image shape.

Did You Know?

You can automatically rename a batch of your digital photo files using ThumbsPlus's Auto Rename command. You can choose a prefix and a suffix as well as add incrementing numbers. This useful feature enables you to add more meaning to your filenames. You can also set the filename to be automatically used as a keyword, which enables you to perform keyword queries using just parts of the filename.

ORGANIZE
your digital photos

One of the greatest challenges in organizing your digital photos is to manage images that are stored on multiple drives, on networks, and on removable media, all from the same image manager — and to have all the images accessible at the same time. Using ThumbsPlus, you can manage images on multiple drives on one PC or one or more drives on some networks.

You can also create thumbnail images and build ThumbsPlus database information on digital photos stored on removable media and external drives.

When you remove an external drive, the thumbnails and database information remain inside the Offline Disks folder. Likewise, you can create thumbnail images and database information for digital photos on a CD-ROM. When the CD-ROM is not in the drive, you can view the thumbnails and database information in the Offline CD-ROMs folder.

As the storage requirements for digital photographers grow, these features become more useful for managing, organizing, and archiving digital photos on a variety of drives and media.

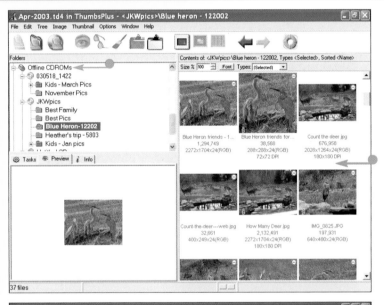

VIEW FILES IN OFFLINE STORAGE

● After creating thumbnails for removable media such as a CD-ROM, ThumbsPlus saves the thumbnails and associated information in an offline CD-ROMs folder.

● You can view thumbnails for offline media without inserting the media in a drive.

● Galleries are logical containers that contain thumbnails stored in a database, but not the full images themselves.

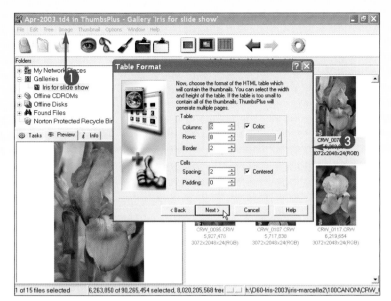

CREATE A WEB PAGE OF SELECTED IMAGES

1 Click Image.

2 Click Web Page Wizard.

An easy-to-use wizard appears, which enables you to customize a Web page to suit your needs.

3 Follow the steps of the wizard to create your Web page.

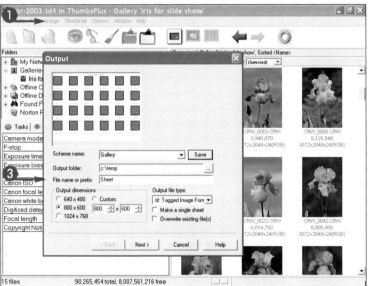

CREATE A CONTACT SHEET

1 Click Image.

2 Click Contact Sheets.

An easy-to-use wizard appears, which enables you to customize the contact sheet's size and layout to suit your needs.

3 Follow the steps of the wizard to create your contact sheet.

TIP

Did You Know?

ThumbsPlus's Gallery feature enables you to save disk space while being able to view thumbnails of the same digital photo in multiple folders. For example, you can save all the digital photos from a trip to Europe in a single folder. You can then create separate gallery folders for landscapes, cities, seascapes, and castles. By right-clicking a group of landscape photos in the Europe folder, you can add them to the landscape gallery. You can do the same for all the city, seascape, and castle photos in the Europe folder. This lets you open a single folder and view all the thumbnails for a single subject, no matter what folder contains the original digital photo file — all while having only a single copy of the file.

Share digital photos with
AOL INSTANT MESSENGER

Instant messengers (*IMs*) are software applications that enable you to exchange text messages in real time with other people on the Internet who have compatible IM software. As soon as you type a message and click the Send button, the message displays on the screen of those with whom you are chatting. They can then type messages and send replies back to you. IMs allow a much more interactive way to communicate than the slower e-mail. You can also create a chat room where you can invite multiple people to join in the chat.

Besides messaging capability, many of the more popular IMs have features that enable you to send a file, which means that you can easily send digital photo files. Sharing your digital photos while chatting about them is a wonderful way not only to share your photos with others, but also for you to get feedback.

Although AOL's Instant Messenger is one of the more popular IMs, you can use other versions like ICQ (www.icq.com) and MSN Messenger (www. microsoft.com).

① Sign in and initiate a chat with a buddy.

② Click File.

③ Click Send File.

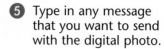

The Send File dialog box appears.

④ Click File to launch the file browser, in which you select the digital photo file.

⑤ Type in any message that you want to send with the digital photo.

⑥ Click Send.

92

DIFFICULTY LEVEL

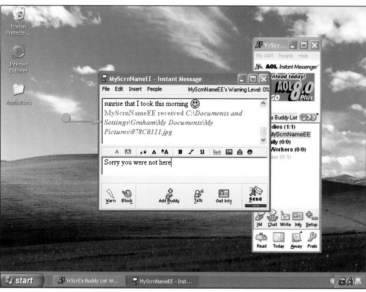

● The AOL Instant Message text window shows that the digital photo was sent.

TIPS

Did You Know?

AOL Instant Messenger is available for those that have paid for and have subscribed to the AOL service. Plus, AOL offers a free version that is available to non-AOL subscribers. You can download the free version from the AOL Web site (www.aim.com). After downloading the software, you can install it, register a screen name, and be chatting within a few minutes.

Caution!

You should be careful whom you accept digital photos from while chatting; you may accept and view a file that you would rather not have seen. The Preferences dialog box offers options to prevent others from sending you digital photos unless you accept them.

ARCHIVE
your digital photo collection to a DVD

Occasionally, a hard drive fails. The older your hard drive is, the more likely it is to fail. To avoid losing all or part of your digital photo collection, you should keep your photos well organized with an image manager and have a procedure in place for periodically *archiving,* or copying, them to another hard drive or to removable media such as a CD or DVD.

One of the easiest and safest ways to archive your digital photos is to burn, or write, them to a DVD. To do that you need a *DVD burner* — a DVD

drive that both reads and writes DVD discs — and you will need software to manage the process. One excellent software product for archiving digital photos to a DVD is Roxio Easy CD & DVD Creator. It is a feature-rich product that enables you to easily archive just a few files or many files that require multiple DVD discs. It also comes with software for printing disc labels and jewel and DVD case inserts.

Turn to Task #91 to organize your photos with an image manager.

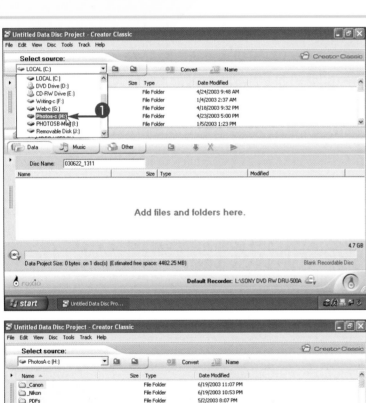

① Click the drive and folder containing the files that you want to archive.

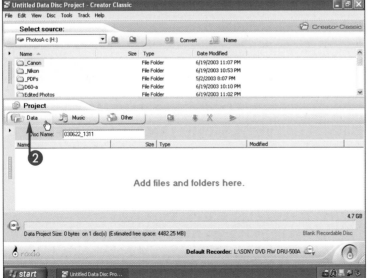

② Click the Data tab to select the record mode.

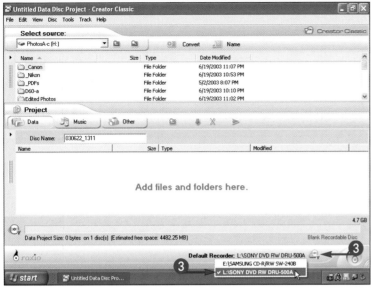

DIFFICULTY LEVEL

③ Click the Default Recorder button and select the DVD drive.

④ Drag one or more folders or files from the Source window to the Project window.

Did You Know?

A DVD holds 4.7GB of digital photos or slightly more than seven CDs. Using a 3-megapixel camera to shoot in the RAW format, you can archive around 1,500 digital photos or the equivalent of about 40 rolls of 36-exposure film on a single DVD.

Caution!

Because it is not certain how long a DVD disc will safely store your digital photos and because a single scratch can prevent you from retrieving your photos, you should take all precautions to protect your archives. It is wise to purchase two different brands of quality DVDs and make two copies when you archive your photos — using one of each brand. This procedure may help prevent you from losing photos on defective media.

ARCHIVE
your digital photo collection to a DVD

When choosing a DVD burner and DVD discs, you must be careful to choose the right format. What is the right format? Unfortunately, drive and media manufacturers are engaged in a standards war, so there are multiple competing formats in the marketplace. Some of the more common formats include DVD-R, DVD+R, DVD-RW, and DVD+RW; then there are also DVD-Video and DVD-RAM.

When choosing a format to archive your digital photographs, you may want to make sure that you choose a drive that allows you to write digital video

slideshows to view on your computer or TV screen. Several manufacturers are making the choice easier by offering DVD burners that can write in multiple formats. To learn about creating a slideshow to view on a DVD player, see Task #97.

Even though there are competing DVD formats, there is not a good reason *not* to buy a DVD burner for archiving your digital photographs. DVD burners are currently one of the best ways to archive your digital photos for safekeeping.

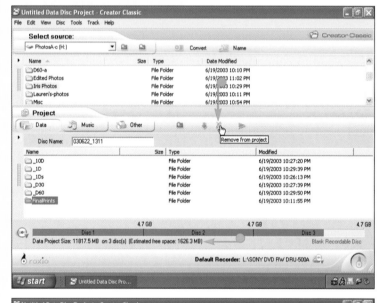

● The Disc Info bar shows how many discs are needed and the available space.

Note: Large digital photo collections may need to be archived to more than one disc.

● You can click a folder or file and then click the Remove from Project button to remove that folder or file from the list of items to be copied.

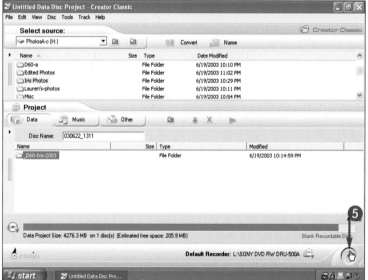

5 Click the Record button.

The Record Setup dialog box appears.

6 Click here and select a write speed.

7 Click here to set the number of copies.

8 Make sure that you have a DVD-R in your DVD-ROM drive.

9 Click OK to begin recording.

The Burn Disc Progress dialog box shows the percentage of completion and the estimated time to complete recording.

TIPS

Caution!

Some early DVD drives and DVD-burning software may write to discs in a format that cannot be read by some of the more current DVD drives. Be careful to use a DVD drive and software that will enable you to read your discs in new DVD drives and on computers with current operating systems.

Did You Know?

DVD drives require firmware and a driver. If you are having problems with your DVD drive, you should check the vendor's Web site for new drivers or firmware. Vendors usually provide easy-to-follow instructions for downloading and installing both the drivers and firmware. When downloading the drivers, make sure to select the correct one for your operating system.

Create a
PDF SLIDESHOW

One of the more fun ways to share photos is to create and view them in a slideshow on a computer screen. You can use many applications to create slideshows. Adobe Photoshop Elements enables you to quickly and easily create a PDF slideshow. A *PDF* (portable document format) is a special file that can be read only using Adobe Acrobat or the free Adobe Acrobat Reader. You can view PDF files on just about all computers, including PCs and Macintoshes. So, you can create a slideshow using a PC or Mac and

share it with anyone, no matter what computer he or she is using.

After you have created a PDF slideshow, all the photos and the settings that you selected for playback are contained in a single file. One of the significant advantages of sharing your digital photos in PDF format is that there are a number of useful features built into Acrobat Reader that allow the images to be exported, edited, printed, and so on.

CREATE A SLIDESHOW

❶ In Elements Organizer, click Create.

The Creation Setup dialog box appears.

❷ Click Slide Show.

❸ Click OK.

The Select a Slide Show Format page appears.

❹ Click Simple Slide Show.

❺ Click OK.

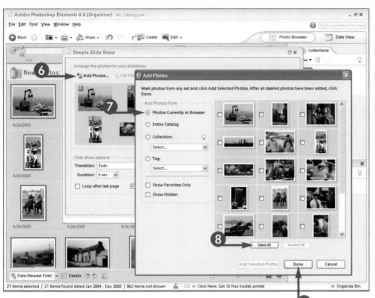

The Simple Slide Show dialog box appears.

6 Click Add Photos.

The Add Photos dialog box appears.

7 Click to select the source of the photos.

8 Click Select All to select all the photos.

9 Click Done.

You are returned to the Simple Slide Show dialog box.

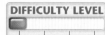

DIFFICULTY LEVEL

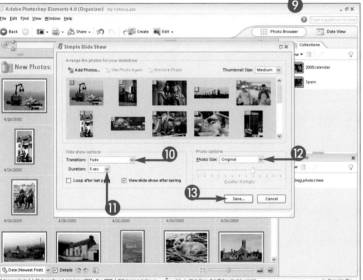

10 Click here and select the transition style to determine how a slide replaces the preceding slide.

11 Click here and select the slide duration time.

12 Click here and select the photo size.

13 Click Save to choose a folder and filename to use to save the slideshow.

The slideshow is generated and displayed in Adobe Acrobat.

Note: The slideshow is now ready to be played or e-mailed.

TIPS

Did You Know?

To view Acrobat slideshows created with Adobe Photoshop Elements, you need a copy of Adobe Acrobat or the free Acrobat Reader. You can download a free copy of Adobe Acrobat Reader at www.adobe.com/products/acrobat/readermain. html. When using Acrobat Reader, you can easily export pictures, export and edit pictures, print pictures, order prints online, and order photo objects online by simply clicking the Picture Tasks button in Acrobat Reader.

Did You Know?

An Acrobat-based slideshow is easy to create and easy to share because there is only a single file instead of one file for each photo plus additional files for a slideshow program and slideshow settings.

Create a
DIGITAL PHOTO ALBUM

You can create the digital equivalent of a photo album with realistic flipping pages with one of E-Book Systems's FlipAlbum products, available at www.flipalbum.com. You can choose from multiple versions of FlipAlbum. FlipAlbum Standard automatically organizes your photos into realistic page-flipping albums that you can view on a PC and share on the Internet. FlipAlbum Suite has extra features that enable you to share your albums on CDs or to play them on some DVD players. FlipAlbum Pro offers all the features of the other two products plus a few more features, including a CD password option, image encryption, watermark capabilities, and a print lock feature to control how images are printed. Mac FlipAlbum is for a Macintosh.

When you create an album, FlipAlbum automatically creates a front and back cover, thumbnail image pages to be used as a table of contents, and an index. Images can be ordered based on the filenames, or you can click and drag the thumbnail images to order them as you want them.

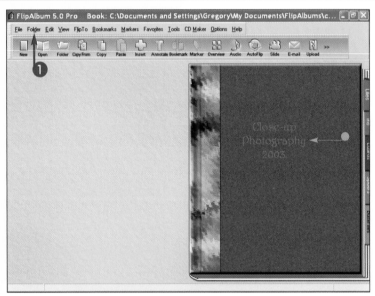

① Click Folder ➪ Open Folder.

The Open Folder dialog box appears.

② Select a folder of photos to be made into a digital photo album.

③ Click OK.

FlipAlbum automatically creates a flip album based on the default settings.

● You can add cover title text with the Annotations tool.

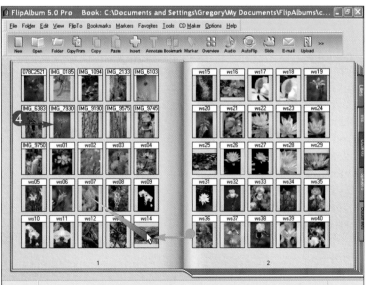

Thumbnails are automatically generated and placed at the front of the album.

● To change the viewing order of the images, you can click and drag and drop the thumbnails.

④ To view a full-size image on an album page, click its thumbnail.

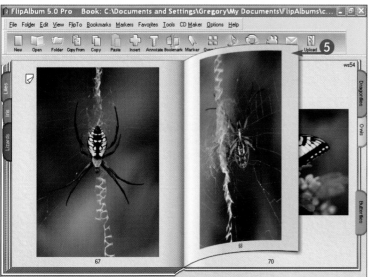

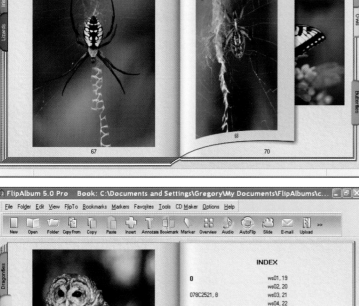

To add a tab, you can right-click the selected page, click Bookmarks ➪ Add, and then type in the tab text and choose a color.

⑤ To turn a page, click in the upper corner of the page to view a flipping page effect.

DIFFICULTY LEVEL

⑥ To view the index, go to the back of the album.

FlipAlbum automatically creates a clickable index at the end of each album when a folder is opened.

Did You Know?

You can further customize a FlipAlbum by selecting a different cover style or by choosing your own cover color, cover image, texture, and binding. You can also choose the color and texture of the pages, the margins, and how the pages "flip." You can add background music and set the entire album to flip automatically. You can add text to each page in the font style and color of your choice, and you can even add a link to a specified Web page.

Apply It!

You can upload your FlipAlbums to E-Book Systems's Web site specifically for sharing FlipAlbums at www.fliplibrary.com.

Create a
WEB PHOTO GALLERY

If you want to make your photos available to anyone in the world who has a computer and a connection to the Internet, you can create an online photo gallery. To create an online photo gallery, you typically need digital photos sized and optimized for use on the Internet, thumbnail photos sized and optimized for use on the Internet, and HTML-based pages (Web pages) with links to the digital photos and thumbnails. Creating all of this without a tool such as Adobe Photoshop Elements is a tedious and time-consuming process.

Using the Adobe Photoshop Elements Web Photo Gallery feature, you can have your online gallery up and running in just a few minutes. Before you run the Web Photo Gallery feature, you should first prepare your digital photos and create a folder in which to put all the images. You should then select these images in Elements Organizer. Although you can use the Web Photo Gallery feature to automatically size and compress each digital photo, you may get better results sizing and compressing each digital photo with the Save for Web command (see Task #71).

CREATE A WEB GALLERY

① In Photoshop Elements Organizer, click Create.

The Creation Setup dialog box appears.

② Click Web Photo Gallery.

③ Click OK.

The Adobe Web Photo Gallery dialog box appears.

④ Click Add.

The Add Photos dialog box appears.

⑤ Click Photos Currently in Browser.

⑥ Click Select All.

⑦ Click Done.

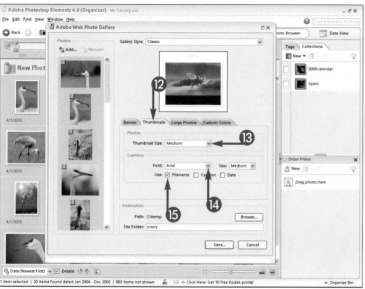

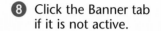

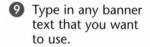

You are returned to the Adobe Web Photo Gallery dialog box.

⑧ Click the Banner tab if it is not active.

⑨ Type in any banner text that you want to use.

⑩ Click Browse and choose a destination folder.

⑪ Type in a short site folder name.

⑫ Click the Thumbnails tab to select thumbnails.

⑬ Click here and select a thumbnail size.

⑭ Click here and select the font.

⑮ Click to check the Filename box if you want to include the filename below each thumbnail.

TIPS

Did You Know?

Most Internet service providers offer you 10MB or more of personal Web space that you can use for your digital photo gallery. Check with your service provider to learn more about the file transfer tools that it offers and how to upload your digital photo gallery. Often, you can find this information on your Internet service provider's Web pages.

Did You Know?

The Adobe Photoshop Elements Web Photo Gallery feature can automatically place a caption under each photo on each Web page. Use the File ➪ File Info command in Photoshop Elements Editor to add a caption in the Caption box for each digital photo file.

Create a
WEB PHOTO GALLERY

Many photographers worry about having their digital photos stolen from online photo galleries and used without payment or permission. Although this is a reasonable concern because it does happen, small digital photo files are not all that useful for most commercial purposes. If you keep all your posted images small, with the maximum size of less than 400 pixels, you are not likely to suffer any great loss.

You can take steps to prevent an image from being

copied, or you can add a copyright or watermark to online images so that they can be tracked and identified. However, the effort that it takes to add this extra protection is generally not worth it because there are ways around each different approach. If you have good reasons for not wanting your digital photos copied, you should not post them to a Web page on the Internet.

⑯ Click the Large Photos tab.

⑰ If you want your digital photos resized, click to check the Resize Photos box and enter the size and quality.

⑱ Click to check the Filename box if you want to display the filename.

● You can also add a caption and the date.

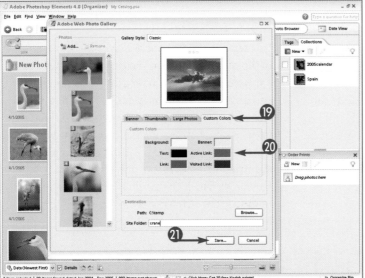

⑲ Click the Custom Colors tab.

⑳ Click in these boxes to choose custom colors for the Web gallery.

㉑ Click Save.

Elements begins the automatic generation of the Web pages, thumbnails, and any image resizing that is required.

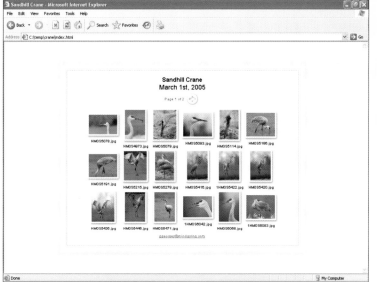

VIEW THE WEB GALLERY

Your Web gallery appears like this when using Microsoft Internet Explorer.

TRANSFER THE FILES

To upload the folders, images, and HTML pages to the Internet, you need to use file transfer software such as WS_FTP Pro or CuteFTP.

1 Click the folder to upload.

2 Click the destination folder on your Web site.

3 Click the Upload button.

Your files are uploaded.

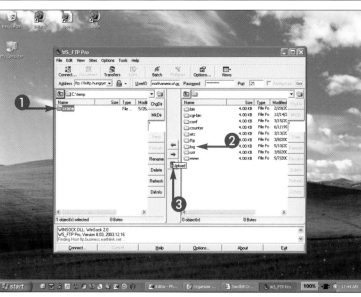

TIPS

Did You Know?

GlobalSCAPE's CuteFTP (www.globalscape.com) is one of the most popular file-transfer software tools used for uploading Web pages and images to an Internet sever. You can download a trial version from the vendor's Web page.

Did You Know?

You can change the graphics and the layout of any of the more than 30 preset Web page styles that are supplied with Adobe Photoshop Elements. You can find a separate folder in the \Photoshop Elements 4.0\shared_assets\webcontactssheet folder for each of the styles. To modify a style, first copy the contents of the folder containing the style that you want to a new folder with a different name. Then edit or replace the images or modify the HTML code with an HTML editor.

Create a
VIDEO SLIDESHOW

People create slideshows for many reasons. Maybe you have just returned from an overseas trip with lots of great photos, and you want to share them with friends and family. Or maybe you have dozens of flower or antique car photos that you would like to share. You may even want to create a slideshow featuring your children or your parents over the years. Whatever the reason, there are many ways to both create and present slideshows.

One of the most useful software products to use to create slideshows on CDs and DVDs is Adobe

Photoshop Elements. Using the Photoshop Elements Slide Show Editor, you can create slideshows that you can view on a computer screen or on a TV that is connected to a DVD player if you have used an appropriate disc format.

An advantage of using a DVD player and a TV for viewing your slideshows is that you can control each slide with the DVD player control, which enables you to go forward or backward, or go to a main menu to select another slideshow.

① In Photoshop Elements Organizer, select all the images that you want to use.

② Click Create.

The Creation Setup dialog box appears.

③ Click Slide Show.

④ Click OK.

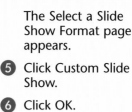

The Select a Slide
Show Format page
appears.

⑤ Click Custom Slide
Show.

⑥ Click OK.

The Slide Show Preferences dialog box
appears.

⑦ Click here and select how long each
image will be displayed.

⑧ Click here and select a slide transition
effect.

⑨ Click OK.

Did You Know?

Video CDs (VCDs) are CD-recordable discs containing audio, video, and still images encoded in the
highly compressed MPEG (moving pictures experts group) format. The VCD format offers lower-quality
images than either the SVCD or DVD formats. Image resolution of full-motion video typically falls below
standard VHS videotape, but still images display clearly.

Super video CDs (SVCDs) offer better image and sound quality than VCDs, but are not as good as
DVDs. However, SVCDs are a good choice for photographers because they represent an acceptable
compromise between inexpensive media and high-resolution images.

A DVD is a DVD-recordable disc that can be played in most standalone DVD players and computer
DVD-ROM drives. The DVD format holds the most content and has the highest image quality.

Create a
VIDEO SLIDESHOW

Just because CD burners, DVD burners, and set-top DVD players are an evolving technology, there is no reason why you should not enjoy the benefits of this new technology now. Carefully check documentation and consult knowledgeable sales staff when purchasing new hardware and media and read the documentation that came with products you already have.

Each of the many types of discs and file formats has advantages and disadvantages. If you have only a CD burner, it is possible that you can use it to create

a VCD or SVCD featuring a photo slideshow that can be viewed on a computer with a CD-ROM reader or on a newer DVD player.

To output a DVD slideshow, you must have a DVD burner and DVD-recordable discs (DVD-R/RWs or DVD+R/RWs). For a VCD or SVCD slideshow, you will need a CD burner and CD-R/RWs. Picking the right disc for the CD or DVD reader or set-top DVD player is as easy as reading the manuals or checking with the vendor.

The Slide Show Editor appears with the photos that were loaded from Organizer.

⑩ Click in the Extras palette to add effects, clip art, text, or voice narration.

⑪ Click here to change the time that the slide is displayed.

⑫ Click to check this box to enable pan and zoom.

⑬ Click one of the handles to drag the start box to where you want the pan or zoom to begin.

⑭ Click here to set the end box.

⑮ Click Preview to preview the resulting effect.

⑯ Click Output Slide Show to view all the output options.

The Slide Show Output dialog box appears.

⑰ Click Burn to Disc.

⑱ Click DVD to create a DVD slideshow.

⑲ Click OK to begin the process of writing the slideshow to the disc.

The Burn dialog box appears.

⑳ Click OK.

● The burn-to-DVD process begins, and a status bar indicates the percentage that is completed.

After the disc has been burned, it will eject and be ready to be played in a DVD player.

TIPS

Caution!

Older set-top DVD players may not be able to play either the VCD or SVCD discs. Some of the newer model set-top DVD players may have problems playing a CD-R disc, but will play a CD-RW disc.

Did You Know?

When you create a video slideshow using Adobe Photoshop Elements Slide Show Editor, you can add digital video clips, music, and multiple slideshows. You can also create your own title screen with selectable menu options similar to those generally found in commercially produced DVD movies; this enables you to have more than one slideshow on a DVD.

Create a
PHOTO CALENDAR

Everyone needs at least one calendar. Using Adobe Photoshop Elements, you can easily create calendars that display your photographs while providing 12 months' worth of calendar pages for keeping track of events. Creating a calendar is as easy as following the steps in the Create a Wall Calendar Wizard. You have a choice of several different styles, including styles for both horizontal and vertical pages, and you can display up to 13 photos, including one photo for the cover and one for each month. If you choose to

add captions below each photo, you can do so by adding the captions that you want to the image file.

After you have created your photo calendar, you can print it out on your own desktop photo printer, or you can use an online printing service.

Photo calendars make excellent gifts. The next time that you need to give a gift, consider making a photo calendar customized for the recipient using your photographs.

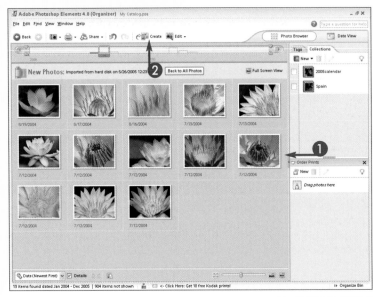

① In Photoshop Elements Organizer, select 13 photos that you want to use.

Note: *You need 13 photos if you want to have an image on the cover.*

② Click Create.

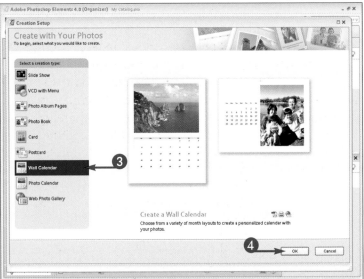

The Creation Setup dialog box appears.

③ Click Wall Calendar.

④ Click OK.

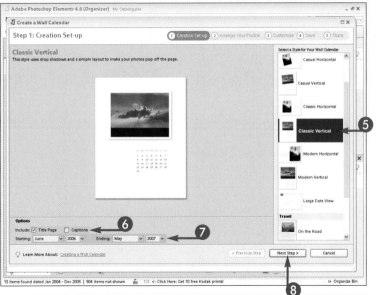

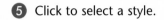
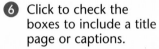
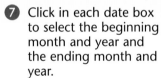

The Create a Wall Calendar Wizard appears.

❺ Click to select a style.

❻ Click to check the boxes to include a title page or captions.

❼ Click in each date box to select the beginning month and year and the ending month and year.

❽ Click Next Step.

The Step 2: Arrange Your Photos page appears.

❾ Click and drag the photos to place them in the order that you want.

❿ Click Next Step.

Did You Know?

You can have photo captions printed below each photo. Place a check mark in the Captions box in the Creation Set-up step of the Create a Wall Calendar Wizard and then enter captions in the digital photo files. To enter captions into the digital photo files using Photoshop Elements Editor, click File ⇨ File Info to open the File Info dialog box. Then type the caption in the Caption box and save the file.

Did You Know?

You can use other software products to create a photo calendar, including Microsoft Word. You can download several Microsoft Word style sheets from the Microsoft Web site at officeupdate.Microsoft.com/templategallery. You can also download the Snapfish Photo Wizard at www.snapfish.com/photowizard and use the wizard to order prints online from Snapfish. Shutterfly (www.shutterfly.com) also offers a service for printing photo calendars.

Create a
PHOTO CALENDAR

Adobe Photoshop Elements enables you to create a wide variety of photo-based print projects. In addition to creating calendars, you can make greeting cards, photo albums, and much more with a simple click of a button. Adobe Photoshop Elements also enables you to retouch, crop, and resize photos. This relatively low-priced software even provides tools for sharing your favorite photos with friends and loved ones online, including built-in templates for creating a Web photo gallery.

You do not have to use Adobe Photoshop Elements to create your own photo calendars. Most imaging software vendors sell similar software, including Ulead Photo Explorer, Broderbund Calendar Creator, and Microsoft Picture It!. The market offers programs that are as basic or as sophisticated as your particular needs. So now that you have taken, enhanced, and archived wonderful digital photos, you can invest in a calendar application and share them in a way that is not only fun but very practical.

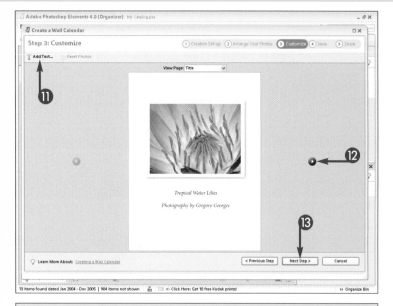

The Step 3: Customize page appears.

⑪ Click Add Text to add text.

⑫ Click here to change pages.

⑬ Click Next Step.

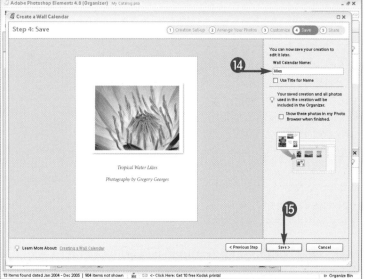

The Step 4: Save page appears.

⑭ Type a name for your wall calendar.

⑮ Click Save to save the project.

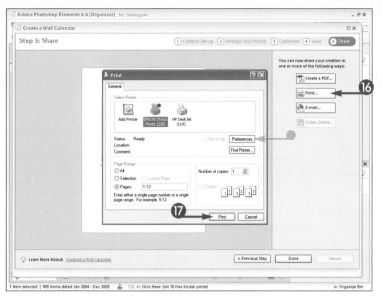

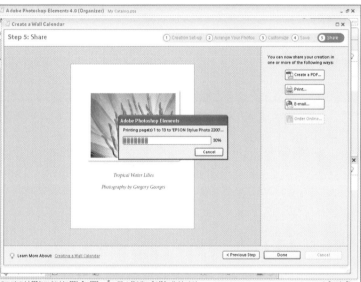

The Step 5: Share page appears.

⑯ Click Print.

The Print dialog box appears.

● You can click Preferences to choose any additional settings that are appropriate for your printer.

⑰ Click Print.

Your calendar begins to print.

Did You Know?

You can create a PDF file instead of printing the calendar to your own desktop printer. In the Step 5: Share part of the Create a Wall Calendar Wizard, click Create a PDF. Then you can select settings to optimize the file for viewing onscreen, for printing, or for full resolution. This is a nice feature if you want to create a calendar, add events to it using Adobe Acrobat, and share it with others. If you use the Optimize for Printing setting, you can add dates and then provide the file on a CD to others so that they can print out their own calendar using high-resolution images. Or you can create a 2.5MB file that is optimized for viewing onscreen and can be downloaded from a Web page.

Create a
PHOTO GREETING CARD

The next time that you need a greeting card, you can make your own personalized card especially for the recipient using one or more of your photos. As you work through each step of the Create a Card Wizard, your steps are automatically saved in a file so that you can quickly make another copy or modify an existing card to create a new one.

One of the strengths of Adobe Photoshop Elements is that the product is designed so that you can download new templates or styles for many of the

creation types when they become available. You can also use various online services such as MyPublisher print services and Shutterfly. After you have signed up for one of these services, you can use them as quickly as you can complete your digital photo projects. To see if new services are available, click Edit ➪ Preferences ➪ Services and then click Updated Creations. If new services are available, they will be integrated into Adobe Photoshop Elements.

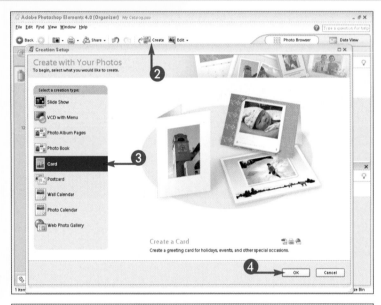

① Select an image that you want to use using Photoshop Elements Organizer.

② Click Create.

The Creation Setup dialog box appears.

③ Click Card.

④ Click OK.

The Create a Card Wizard appears.

⑤ Click a style to use.

⑥ Click Next Step.

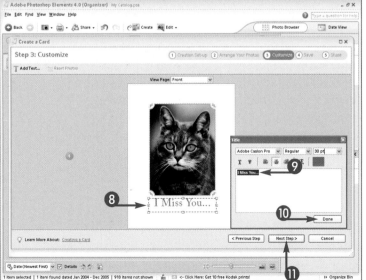

The Step 2: Arrange Your Photos page appears.

⑦ Click Next Step.

The Step 3: Customize page appears.

⑧ Double-click on the text to open the Title dialog box.

⑨ Type your greeting.

⑩ Click Done.

⑪ Click Next Step.

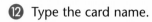

The Step 4: Save page appears.

⓬ Type the card name.

⓭ Click Save.

The greeting card project is saved to your hard drive.

DIFFICULTY LEVEL

The Step 5: Share page appears.

⓮ Click Print.

The Print dialog box appears.

● You can click Preferences to choose any additional settings that are appropriate for your printer.

⓯ Click Print.

Your card begins to print.

Did You Know?

The Adobe Photoshop Elements Create a Card Wizard makes it easy for you to print greeting cards with your own desktop printer. You can also publish a card as a PDF file or as an attachment for e-mail; plus, you can save the card to a CD or order the card to be printed professionally from an online service vendor.

Did You Know?

Many stationery vendors make greeting card paper and matching envelopes especially for use with inkjet printers. You can find tinted, glossy, embossed, mat, and many other varieties in a pre-scored format for easy and accurate folding. Check your local office supply store or order online from www.staples.com or www.officedepot.com.

Create a
PHOTOMONTAGE

A popular thing to do with printed photographs is to cut them up and creatively place and glue them on a single board, making a photo collage. The collage technique is good for assembling a group of photos taken on a vacation, a family get-together, or a sporting event. However, the process of creating a collage in this manner takes some skill and lots of time.

In sharp contrast, making a photomontage with Adobe Photoshop Elements is both easy and fun. Not only are all the photos printed on a single page,

which is why it is called a *photomontage* instead of a *collage,* but the process enables you to size and easily crop each image as needed.

Before you begin placing the digital photos on a new blank document, you should first roughly size the photos so that you minimize the work that it takes to resize them as you place them. When you have resized each photo, you can begin the simple process of dragging, dropping, placing, and sizing each digital photo.

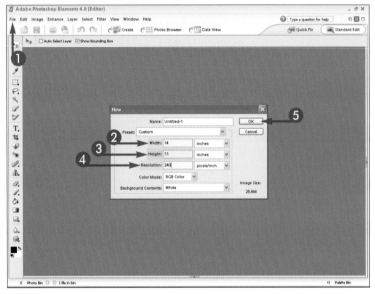

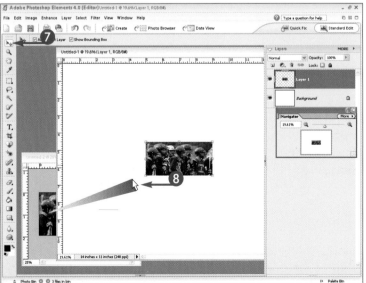

CREATE A PHOTOMONTAGE

① Click File ➪ New.

The New dialog box appears.

② Type in the width, in inches, that you want for the finished photomontage.

③ Type in the height, in inches, that you want for the finished photomontage.

④ Specify the target printer's optimal resolution.

⑤ Click OK to create a new document.

⑥ Open one or more images to use in the photomontage.

⑦ Click the Move tool.

⑧ Drag the images to the new document.

The images appear in the new document window.

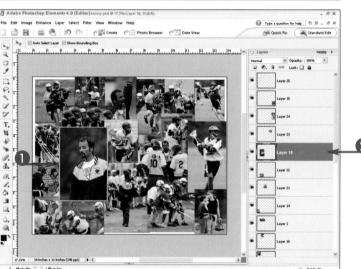

9 Repeat steps **6** to **8** until you have added all the photos to the new document.

10 Click Auto Select Layer if it is not already checked.

11 Drag images to where you want them in the new document window.

DIFFICULTY LEVEL

PLACE AN IMAGE IN FRONT OF ANOTHER

1 Click the image to highlight it in the Layers palette.

2 Click the highlighted layer in the Layers palette and drag it up or down until the layer order is as you want it.

TIPS

Did You Know?

When arranging photos in a photomontage, you can resize any image to fit the available space. Click an image to select it and then click and drag one of the handles to size the image. To maintain the image's aspect ratio, press Shift while adjusting the image size.

Did You Know?

When you have completed placing, sizing, and ordering all the images in a photomontage, you can easily add a shadow line to each photo to add depth to your work. Simply click each layer in the Layers palette and then click your choice of shadow from the Drop Shadows styles found in the Layer Styles palette.

Index

Numbers

Index

Index

Index

Index

Index

Index

Index

Want more simplified tips and tricks?

Take a look at these

All designed for visual learners—just like you!

Read Less—Learn More®

HTUTW 775
G351
2ED

GEORGES, GREGORY.
DIGITAL PHOTOGRAPHY

TUTTLE
06/07

0-7645-03619-2   0-7645-2580-8   0-7645-4393-8

Visual
An Imprint of ⓦ **WILEY**
Now you know.